WORDS from GOD

Published by
Words from God,
17 Orient Street,
Batemans Bay, N.S.W. 2536, Australia.

Telephone:
National (044) 729559
International +61 44 729559
Facsmile:
National (044) 726749
International +61 44 726749

ISBN 0 646 15829 5

Ireland
66 Landscape Park
Churchtown
Dublin 14
Telephone: (01) 628 7348

United Kingdom
2 Barling Road
Great Wakering
Essex SS3 0QB
Telephone: (0702) 582 335

"No matter your age, no matter your state in life, these messages can help you to grow closer to Me, your Heavenly Father, and do My will in everything you do. My children today I speak to you all, men and women, young and old, priests, religious, and laity. I have chosen this young boy in the middle of nowhere to receive My messages and I have entrusted to him the mission of spreading the messages.

These words are from wisdom itself. I am God, I am Wisdom. You must have faith in these messages and live them out. They don't oppose the church, they support the church; they support the Pope especially. And these messages are directly linked to the work John Paul II,(the chosen Pope for these times) has been entrusted with.

My children accept this boy into your homes, support his cause, for I am the Lord your God. (.....)

My children return to the sacraments and return to living lives of prayer.

I have spoken to this young boy so that he can share it with all of My children. I am the Lord your God; I have used an extraordinary way to bring you back to the ordinary things of your faith, like the *sacraments and prayer*.

My children I love you all and My delight is in being with you. Receive these words, they are 'Words from God,' but more than that, you must *all* start to live these messages.

Now is the time, you are the person, and change is the need. Soften your heart today so that you can love Me more. Read, believe and live."

9/6/93

Words From God

The decree of the Congregation for the Propagation of the faith, A.A.S.58, 1186 (Approved by Pope Paul VI on October 14, 1966) states that the Nihil Obstat and Imprimatur are no longer required on publications that deal with private revelations, provided that they contain nothing contrary to faith and morals.

The publisher recognizes and accepts that the final authority regarding the events described in this book rests with the Holy See of Rome, to whose judgement we willingly submit.

The Publisher

Introduction

On the 7th of April 1993, as I knelt beside my bed saying my evening prayers I found myself at what seemed to be a crossroad in my life. I had many unanswered questions in my mind and I desperately yearned for the gift of discernment, believing that it was in doing God's will that I would find my happiness.

Unresolved, I finished my prayer in a hurry and climbed into bed. As always I said the Hail Mary three times, one that Our Lady might take care of me during the night, one for my family and friends, and one for society. Then I reached for my walkman thinking I might find some comfort in the words of a song.

As I reached for my walkman I felt a strong external presence and a feeling that urged me not to pick up my walkman. I ignored that and reached for it all the same and as I put the headphones on, I had a similar feeling only this time it was twice as powerful. I ignored it.

Finally, I turned the walkman on and after two or three seconds of music I had that same feeling again, but this time it was unmistakable, I knew that this was something I had never experienced before. And so I got out of bed, knelt down and I put myself in the presence of God. During that day and throughout this experience I felt God was asking something of me, yet, I couldn't pinpoint it. I felt God wanted to speak to me. So kneeling there in my bedroom I said "I am listening". All in an instant, I heard what I now know to be the voice of God the Father, speak to me.

Over the three months following that evening, the contents of this book have been dictated to me by God the Father,

Jesus, and Mary, with the never failing assistance of the Holy Spirit.

A renewed life of prayer by reflecting on these messages daily has brought me a happiness that is not affected by the fluctuations of emotions or circumstances. A happiness that is true.

God the Father has stated that through these messages, He does not only speak to me but to each person who cares to open their heart and read them. I pray that you also are able to find Christ more in your life, where you are now, by reading, reflecting, and praying about these messages.

I will never forget the early April evening on which this chapter of my life began and I think the most valuable thing I have learnt since then is that "all the answers are in the tabernacle" and that prayer is all powerful.

Take your time to read through these messages and as you go through them pause at every occasion you feel appropriate and ask Our Lord for His assistance in putting the messages into effect in your life, or just speak with Him about how a particular message relates to your life.

What is contained in this book is a series of messages that outline a practical way of loving the Lord your God with your whole heart, mind, body, and soul; and your neighbour as yourself, during these times in the world. May God bless the world with peace and each of us with the joy of knowing Christ.

Matthew Kelly.
24th August, 1993.
Feast of St. Bartholomew, Apostle.

1 "Keep doing what you are doing, and believe in yourself, and in Me."

7th April, 1993.

3 "Listen to Me, hear My words, and do My will."

11th April, 1993.

5 "Keep your mind open and trust in Me your Father."

12th April, 1993.

6 "In My time."

12th April, 1993.

7 "Fear comes from Satan."

12th April, 1993.

8 "Pray My son, and you will understand."

12th April 1993.

9 "Remember My son, I am your Father, and I will guide you."

12th April, 1993.

10 "Strength of character comes from prayer."

13th April, 1993.

11 " (.....) you must have strength My son, and follow Me always, with peace and joy, and accept the pain of My way with love."

13th April, 1993.

12 "Do not be afraid, do as I ask and all will be provided."

13th April, 1993.

13 " (.....) Go into the days longing for Me and My will and remember always I am by your side."

14th April, 1993.

14 "When it all comes down to it, what you have done for Me is all that counts."

14th April, 1993.

15 "I said believe in yourself and believe in Me."

14th April, 1993.

16 "When the people around you are weak, you must be strong."

15th April, 1993.

17 "You should love all, those who don't love you in return will be overcome, their hearts will be softened, and in the spirit of My Son Jesus you will win their hearts."

15th April, 1993.

18 "My way is full of thorns and roses, but the love of your Father will get you through. Love. Love all. For love is the answer My son."

15th April, 1993.

19 "You ask Me what you should do. The answer I have placed in your heart."

15th April, 1993.

20 "Music can echo a voice from Heaven or a voice from hell. Let Me use you as an instrument My son."

15th April, 1993.

22 "These words I am sending you are to encourage and to guide you."

15th April, 1993.

24 "Don't worry about what lies far in front of you. Deal with the task I have given you for this moment."

16th April, 1993.

25 "Nothing is beyond Me My son, open yourself to My grace, let Me develop your talents. Trust. Trust and Pray."

16th April, 1993.

27 "My son, don't be discouraged by illness. Accept it as part of My way. Suffer as My Son Jesus did, acceptingly, and I will raise you up. Illness can be fruitful."

16th April, 1993.

28 "Learn to live with people by way of My love. Bring them My love and you will bring them to Me."

17th April, 1993.

29 "My son I have built a fire in your heart. Prayer, the Mass and the Rosary are the logs on the fire and are what will keep the fire burning strong."

17th April, 1993.

30 "The Love of your Father is greater than any force on earth so just trust in Me."

17th April, 1993.

32 "The girl you are looking for can appreciate that you are trying to please Me, your Father, in everything you do. Don't compromise."

18th April, 1993.

33 "Humility My son is the key to sustaining a solid relationship with Me. Remain humble and remember worldly talents are worthless unless offered to Me. Follow your dream, I want for that, but let us follow it together."

18th April, 1993.

34 " (.....) In Me you have, and will always find a way. Nothing is impossible for your Heavenly Father."

18th April, 1993.

36 "As soon as you realise My son, you will leave your ways and follow Mine. You will give up crawling to fly."

18th April, 1993.

37 " It is not for you to worry about those around you. Give them your love, pray for them, and trust in Me your Father. Love, love, love. Show them My love and they will respond to My call."

18th April, 1993.

38 "Peace, My son. Peace of mind, Peace of heart, peace of soul. My Peace."

"My son, these words arc a privilege."

19th April, 1993.

39 "Keep doing what you are doing with the focus always on Me."

19th April, 1993.

40 " (.....) Little by little, My son. What is gained quickly is lost quickly."

19th April, 1993.

42 "Don't worry if you think you are getting nowhere. Only I see the results of the work you do. Keep working and praying. Your work is not done while there are still souls who need help."

20th April, 1993.

43 "My gifts are plentiful to those who open themselves to them."

20th April, 1993.

44 "You are weak. You realise you are weak; good. In Me, My son, is your strength."

20th April, 1993.

45 "Fight on. The battle is long and hard, but real strength comes from your Father in Faith, Hope and Love. Trust."

21st April, 1993.

46 "I want you to do My will for now, the future lies in the future. Trust in Me, your Heavenly Father for whom nothing is impossible."

21st April, 1993.

47 "Love. Love more. It is by love that all is won for your Father in Heaven. It is by love that the world will be united as one."

21st April, 1993.

49 "I am the Lord your God, you shall have no other god. I have wept for you in My Son, I have died for you in My Son.

This is My message: Love Me your God and love all people."

22nd April, 1993.

50 " (.....) The Eucharist is so important for your growth. It is the food on which you will survive."

22nd April, 1993

51 "Show Me that you love Me. (.....)"

22nd April, 1993.

52 "Live what you believe and love to live this way, in Me your Father in Heaven."

22nd April, 1993.

53 "Pray and be patient, My son."

22nd April, 1993.

54 "Your work must be done for Me. No matter what you are doing it should be done well out of love for Me.

By disciplining yourself to work well, you will gain enormous inner strength which will allow you to love Me better in everything else you do."

22nd April, 1993.

55 *Why are people so caught up in worldly things? (Matthew)*

"People are unable to see the beauty of supernatural life, they are unable to see past their own selfish short term desires and as a result find themselves forever thirsty and without peace."

Why are they unable? (Matthew)

"Because they have rejected My grace so often out of ignorance and selfishness. Because they choose self first. They don't know Me, or My Son, or the Spirit. They don't pray."

What should we do? (Matthew)

"Go out into the world tomorrow as the people you were today and start changing little things. Smile, say less and listen more, pray to Me, and trust in Me your Heavenly Father."

22nd April, 1993.

57 Jesus: "I am the life of the world. Where you see laughter and joy, you see Me. Where you find peace, you find Me. Where you find love you find Me.

I am your laughter and joy, your peace and your hope."

22nd April, 1993.

58 "Fear not My son I am with you."

22nd April, 1993.

61"Music is the key."

The key to what? (Matthew)

"We must put a song in everyone's heart. A song of love and then the world will be united in My Son's name, Jesus Christ."

22nd April, 1993.

62 "Yes My son, believe for I am your God."

23rd April, 1993.

63 "Express your love for Me in the way you treat other people and in the work that you do."

23rd April, 1993.

65 "I am here and I hear you My son. It's easy to love those who love you, but you must love all. It's hard I know, but try to open your heart more to those people who don't show you love. Do not be afraid, I am with you."

23rd April, 1993.

66 "You are young and full of energy. Direct this energy towards My will. What you hope and dream for is small compared to what I have planned for you."
   How will I know your will? (Matthew)
"Pray, learn about yourself, and My Son Jesus Christ in the Gospels, and the answers I will place in your heart."

23rd April, 1993.

67 "I sent My Son to save the world. Throughout the ages I have had to rely on few to carry His message, light and love. I ask you to carry His message wherever you go. Make His love the centre of all your relations with people. Make His light shine from you. Let His love find a way into every corner of your body. You ask Me My will. This is My will."

23rd April, 1993.

68 "My son, be good and obedient, faithful and strong and no harm will come to you. Stay in My love and the evil one will not shake you. You have weapons, use them."

23rd April, 1993.

69 *How should we thank you for all you have given us? (Matthew)*
"The way you thank a friend: with stronger friendship. Talk to Me, My children. Share with Me your secrets and your troubles. Let Me share your successes and your joys. I am your Father, I want to be with My children."

24th April, 1993.

70 "Don't divide your heart, give it all to Me and there will be room for all."

24th April, 1993.

71 "Life on earth is a journey. You must have aims and goals for your journey. Otherwise you will not reach the desired end, which of course, is here in Heaven with Me, your Father. Be sure to guard against the wickedness and snares of the devil, who will try to make you believe that to be idle is desirable or deserved. Work increasingly to further your position in your journey, and remember I am by your side always. We are travelling together."

24th April, 1993.

73 "My son, My son, I want for you to love Me with your whole heart, mind and soul, in everything you do. If you do this you will have no trouble discerning what it is I am asking of you for the moment. Then put your whole heart into the moment showing Me that you love Me."

25th April, 1993.

75 "You are no longer to hunger for material possessions. Don't collect them. Don't be attached to them. Your hungry need for them will be extinguished. I am your Father and the provider for the family. I will provide."

25th April, 1993.

76 "Day by day. My way is long and hard and requires perseverance. Pray and you will have the strength to carry on. Love those around you and your strength will be increased.

Accept persecution in My Son's name and you will be rewarded and strengthened.

I am your Father, those who do My work are given the strength and grace to do it. Remember always you are little, I raise you up making you great. Remain always with Me, in My love, and all will be yours that you require to do My work. Be selfless and give yourself up to My will."

26th April, 1993.

77 "You must progress little by little in My love. You progress in My love by the way you work; by the way you play; by the way you conduct friendships; by the way you sacrifice, to show Me that you love Me. My love is thirst quenching, continue to progress."
26th April, 1993.

...s the starting point of your apostolate. Offer
...le, your Father, for different people whom you
a... ...help by bringing them closer to Me.

Do you work well, down to the last detail. The small things done out of love for Me mean much to Me. Then when you are with the people you are trying to help, or indeed anywhere around people, you will affect them and influence them. It's so natural that you should. Your love for Me your Heavenly Father will overflow into others, especially through your smile. Work well and hard, pray, go to Mass, say the Rosary, and do sacrifices. All these will create a love for Me so strong in you that your apostolate will be very fruitful. You will bring people back to the fullness of My love. And people will know Christ has found a home in you."

26th April, 1993.

79 "People are complex beings biologically. But they have taken it upon themselves to complicate their lives by many means, this is the devil's work.

Simplicity is the key to living the life I want you to live. Simplify your life by reducing your attachment to the material world and by trusting in Me, your Heavenly Father who loves and will care for you. Love is all that is important. Faith should rule your lives. And your faith should overflow into a fountain of love for all. Love is simple. Love is My way."

27th April, 1993.

80 "My son the day is only half done. You must fight all the day long to bring My spirit and love into all your activities. This time out of the noise of the world (in prayer*) will give you your strength in this fight. Keep it up."

* *Matthew*
27th April, 1993.

81 "Go now with My love and distribute it to all those who haven't taken this time with Me today to absorb My love and My life. You won't need to mention My name, by the way you act, and by the very nature of your love they will know you are a follower of My Son Christ. They will know that God is dwelling in your heart. (.....)"

27th April, 1993

82 "I am the Master Builder. I have the plans. I merely ask you and your colleagues to lay the bricks. But first you need foundations-prayer, the Mass, the Rosary, sacrifice. These are solid foundations on which to build our house.

Preparation is important for anything, but especially My work. Prepare for doing My work by speaking to Me and telling Me how each friend you are trying to help is progressing. This will give strength to your work and you will see with more clarity what it is you should do. My work is of the upmost importance.

If you love Me you will do My work by sharing My love with those around you. Do you think they are there for no reason?"

28th April, 1993.

83 "Your days are filling, that is good, but be careful not to fill them with fruitless activities which are neither pleasing to Me, or a good use of time.

Your time is a great gift from Me, your Father, but a limited one, use it well. Use it to please Me and further the reign of My Kingdom."

28th April, 1993.

84 " (.....) My son, tonight I call you to My love again. The love of your Heavenly Father is warm, and affectionate, and consistent.

Human love on the other hand is inconsistent and that is why I must be united in, and indeed the centre of, all human love. It is by this, that human love gains consistency and strength in difficult times. And it is by this, that human love is sanctified.

What good is an earthly love if it costs you your inheritance to Heaven?

Young people don't realise how important it is to love Me, so as to love self, so as to love one another truly and selflessly. Lead by example My son."

28th April, 1993.

85 "Change. Life is a process of change. This is all I ask of you. Look at yourself openly and honestly with humility and realise your human weaknesses. And bring them to Me your Heavenly Father, for I make the weak strong. I am your strength. And the way is shown you by My Son, Jesus' example: love."

29th April, 1993.

86 "Today is just the beginning. Each day is a new beginning and what better way to begin than with the Mass."

29th April, 1993.

87 "My kindness is unending, but so many don't realise. They put it down to coincidence, or mystery, or fate, when really it is the kindness of their Heavenly Father's providence.

So too My son you must learn to be kind with your time, your love, and your material possessions, all of which are gifts from Me your Heavenly Father. I have given to you out of kindness and now you also must give kindly. Give of yourself, selflessly, endlessly, as My Son Jesus Christ did. Follow His example of kindness, his example of love."

29th April, 1993.

88 "Begin. Begin. Begin. Pray for others. Primarily, this is how you will help them. This is the best way to start bringing people back to My love. Pray that they might open themselves up to My grace and gifts just a little more each day. And to assist this, soften their hearts by loving them. Show them the warmth of My love."

30th April, 1993.

89 "My son, My son, remember your duties, to your family, to your friends, to Me. Starting with prayer, you have a duty to pray. Speak to Me in prayer and I will guide you in all other activities.

After your duty to people comes your duty to work. You must strive for excellence offering your work to Me for the development of your soul and other souls. Otherwise your work is fruitless and you neglect your duty."

30th April, 1993.

90 "A father on earth plays an important role in a child's development. By the way he acts and the words he speaks, he shows example and the children can choose to follow or ignore that example. I have spoken to you and given you My Son as an example, you can choose to follow or ignore.

That is the freedom I gave all My sons and daughters, but they forget they are sons and daughters of God. They forget the Father who loves them. They neglect to reflect on the most elementary of things: life and where it comes from. I have given you life that you might live it to the fullest.

To do this you must listen and reflect on these words I have given you and do the same with the Bible. Then live following the example I have given you in My Son, Jesus Christ. He is the Way, the Truth and the Life, and the only way to Me, your Heavenly Father."

30th April, 1993.

91 Jesus: "My way is the Truth. I was sent by the Father to install truth on earth, to show all men the way, but they ignore the truth, they ignore Me. Pray today, live by My example of love. Let love guide your actions and you will please My Father and He will grant you eternal life.

If by love you act, then you will be living selflessly and you will be happy. If you are not living by love, for others and for My Father's will, then you will be unhappy. Unhappiness and selfishness go hand in hand, and are what the evil one desires for all men.

Live by love with trust. I have died for you, I shall stay by your side all the way."

1st May, 1993.

92 "Tiredness is natural, laziness is not. I made man to work. Tiredness and laziness can be overcome. You must not become a slave to your body, you must condition it so it becomes a suitable home for Me to live in. A suitable instrument for Me to use.

Conditioning comes from discipline. There is useful and useless disciplining. Mortification and penance are useful forms of disciplining and should be exercised daily, even if only in little ways, to condition the body.

You are a physical and spiritual being. Your physical state is temporal, your spiritual state is eternal. That which lasts forever should reign over that which is temporal. The spirit should lead the body, the body should not lead the spirit."

1st May, 1993.

93 "Today is a day of work. Tomorrow is a day of work. My work is never done. And My work is your work. I use you as My instruments. Love is the secret. If you love Me you will never tire in doing My work well.

Show Me that you love Me in everything you do, everyday. If you are really serious about loving Me, the people around you won't be able to help but notice. My love will be like a light in you, a fire in your heart."

1st May, 1993.

94 "My words are of love, they are gentle but firm. Love has strength and so do My words. When you speak, your words too should be of love. You should be gentle when you speak, because you can cause much damage with your words. By love you will have strength in all you speak and people will realise whose message you bring.

It is not enough just to spread My message by mouth, you must act accordingly. It is here that you have your greatest opportunity to do My work, quietly.

Also you should do sacrifices for those around you and pray that they accept My way and grow to love it. If you speak to them with love they will love you and then they will love Me. For it is by friendship that you will be able to bring people to join the sheepfold. The lost sheep will return by friendship. And friendship is love. So love."

2nd May, 1993.

95 "Quietly, calmly go about doing what you know you ought to be doing, with the minimum of fuss. Don't try to attract attention. If you are trying to live as My Son Christ did, then you will certainly attract attention in today's world.

Don't think that the environment you have to do it in is harsher than that of any that have gone before you, it is not. Just focus on the job at hand, just focus on Me and all will be well. You must trust, it is the key."

2nd May, 1993.

96 "I am a giver. My Son, Jesus was a giver. If you want to follow 'the way' you too must be a giver.

Give all, until you have nothing left to give. Keep nothing for yourself, I your Heavenly Father will provide all you need. So give, your time, your love, your heart, to those who need it. Give what money you can, but be careful with this, many cry out of need, but few are really that needy. And for all those you give to, pray. *Prayer strengthens any gift, and gives true authenticity to any gift.* Give and Pray."

2nd May, 1993.

97 "The end times are near. There must be a sense of urgency about My work by all those who work for Me, but you should never lose your peace and calm and never rush anything.

Do My will, My plan is perfect and allows for all. Don't think these times mean you must take matters into your own hands, no. I will guide you and I will provide each moment necessary to fulfil My plan, and time will not end one minute before this.

But you must have a sense of urgency within you, to drive you, an urgency to love, so that no opportunity to love, serve or share Me is wasted."

3rd May, 1993.

99 "My Word is important. There is nothing old fashion or outdated about it. It is renewed many times throughout the day worldwide in the sacrificing of My Son for all humanity in Holy Mass. My Word is in the Gospels; if you want to love Me you will want to be like Me. I gave you an example in My Son Jesus Christ.

An example of love. This love is reflected in the Gospels, which reflect My Son's life on earth and remain for you to savour and learn from.

My Word is a wonderful gift, appreciate it. Be selfless and you will begin to appreciate the many beautiful gifts I have given you. Appreciate My gifts and you will love them, and they will fill you with love, and you will spread this love throughout the world. Yes, you will spread My love throughout the world."

3rd May, 1993.

100 "You young people are rich, but you squander your wealth. I give you energy incomparable to any other time of your life and you lay idle for much of your time, searching constantly to be entertained in the moment.

So many of you even neglect to pray. Don't wait until you are old to love Me, it may be too late. Love Me now, and use the energy I have given you to love Me."

4th May, 1993.

101 "Consistency and perseverance. These are both so important in love. You won't always feel like loving, but you must always struggle to do your best.

You won't always feel like praying but you must persevere. I am your loving Father in Heaven, and if you only knew how easy it is to talk to Me. It is you that put up the barriers. Tear them down and persevere with your prayer.

It is when times are tough that you show Me that you really love Me. You must struggle always to be consistent in your love. Therefore, you need the supernatural outlook I have granted you, and renew through prayer. Because human love is inconsistent, but My love is consistent. Love and Persevere."

4th May, 1993.

102 "Be sure, be very sure now that you have finally found *'the way'*, but you have a long way to go on your journey. And, *now you are travelling with Me you have nothing to fear,*

all will be provided.

You are My son and I am your Father, it is only natural that I feed you, clothe you and give you a place to rest, both spiritually and in earthly affairs.

In spiritual terms, I fulfil them all in the Mass. I feed you with My Son's precious body, I clothe you with My Word, and I give you a place to take rest from the chaos of the world.

In earthly affairs I have given you many talents, you must strive to use them to the best of your ability and use all the human means available. And realise that it is only with Me that you can do anything. And then trust. I will provide. I will provide opportunities that you could never have imagined for. I am your Father and I love you. Is that not enough?"

4th May, 1993.

103 "My words are soft and gentle, and for the humble. You must work always on being humble, on being the littlest of all. You must open yourself to doing My work and for this you need humility.

If you are to be My instrument you must be humble. The proud cannot love, and to love is all I ask of you. If you want to be with Me you must humble yourself and love."

5th May, 1993.

104 "Your best is all I ask. Don't get discouraged by your human limitations, let them help you to realise how much you need Me.

Then struggle, knowing that I am by your side while you are struggling to do your best in human activities. It is this struggling that will bring you closer to Me, along with prayer.

And, a lifetime full of these results in sanctity. You were born to be a saint."

5th May, 1993.

105 "Words are worthless unless they invoke action. Unless you hear these words and change yourself, your lifestyle and the aim of your life, then these words are worthless.

You must live these words. You must never tire in trying, you will never reach perfection, but that is the beauty of the human state and My love. I only ask that you struggle. So struggle with all your might."

5th May, 1993.

106 "Love is all around you, it is in every person you see, meet or speak about everyday. Even the people you cannot bear to be around it seems, are *full of love.*

You must express your love more by showing interest in them. Not out of duty, but out of love. That person is as important as the next.

Think at the end of each day, who did I treat the worst today? And that is how you have treated Me.

You must love, because you know Me and then they will begin to know Me through you. And the fountain of My love within them will begin to flow again. Love is the answer, love is the task. To love Me you must love all."

6th May, 1993.

107 *"People are precious, each one deserves your undivided attention when you are with them.* Love them as you would like them to love you. Give them the attention you would like to be given yourself.

If you were speaking to a star of any brand, that you admired, you would be fully in the moment. Well in that person I have found a home, in each and every person, when you speak to them you speak to Me."

6th May, 1993.

108 "Never be content, this is a weapon of the devil. You are dust, you have nothing to be proud of, or content with. You are an instrument of My great work. And work you must. Work on!"

6th May, 1993.

109 "You seem intent on living an easy life. Life was never designed to be easy. Even from the first I made man to work, and work you must.

And, furthermore, if you want to follow My Son Jesus Christ, if you want to be like Him, you must suffer like Him. You must be, and will be crucified many times a day, by people who don't believe, by people who don't want to believe.

Accept the cross as Jesus did. Love the cross as Jesus did. And never forget, I am there always, at your side to pick you up if you fall. Love Me, I will not leave you."

"If you think the suffering of carrying the cross, your suffering, is worthless, you haven't stopped to consider the importance of suffering on the cross, the significance."

7th May, 1993.

110 Jesus: "I am your inspiration, love is your motivation."

7th May, 1993.

111 "Sacrifice endlessly, you can never do enough. You bring Me great joy and do much good by sacrificing, good that you never see. But don't be as foolish and naive to believe that your efforts are fruitless.

Think of the fruits Christ My Son's sacrifices brought. If you ensure your sacrifices are in the same spirit they will yield similar fruits.

Similar hidden fruits. Hiddeness is the secret to sacrifice. Don't be like the Pharisees, your reward must be in Heaven."

7th May, 1993.

112 "If you are tired, take rest just as My Son Jesus did when He went into the desert to pray, rest and fast.

Because it is the world that makes you tired. It is not that you are working too hard or fasting too much. It is the world and its lack of balance, warped priorities and the demands it makes upon you.

If you are tired take rest. Get away from it all and rest in My love, preferably for a few moments each day in a church.

The ideas the world propose are warped, rest is not an excuse for laziness."

8th May, 1993.

113 "Children: look at them, study them, then be like them. They are gentle and rough, but they are sincere. They have a real sincerity before the world robs them of their innocence. If you look at children and spend time with them you will learn many things. But you will particularly learn to ask Me,

your Father in Heaven, for things.

Children are dependant, so they need to ask. Realise your dependence and you will realise the importance of that part of your prayer when you ask Me for things.

Children are a fountain of supernatural direction, be with them."

8th May, 1993.

114 "Sexuality is one of the greatest gifts I have given you as a human being. This facility allows you to take part in the creation of a human being, the creation of life. That is indeed beautiful.

The abuse of this gift causes many of the problems in the world, because love is selfless and the only reason for abusing your sexuality is selfishness.

Don't be selfish. Love properly and cleanly. If you are to follow My Son Jesus Christ you will realise the importance of guarding your sexuality.

Give yourself completely to Me. Abandon yourself to My will. Love selflessly and I will look out for you. I will be your God."

8th May, 1993.

115 "Fear not. If you are scared of what the future holds you will be less effective as an instrument of Mine.

You must trust in Me and the plan I have for you. You must concern yourself only with what I ask of you in each moment. *The light will be shed step by step, the doors opened one by one.* Trust."

9th May, 1993.

116 "My will is disclosed step by step."

9th May, 1993.

117 "My son, I am the Way, the Truth and the Life. It is in Me that you will find your direction. Become like Me by reading and listening to the Gospels. See what I do, then do the same. Be like Me because I am meek and humble is My heart.

I was little so that My greatness could be truly recognised. You too must be little so My greatness can be recognised.

Follow Me. Follow Me. Follow Me. I will not lead you into the dark abyss, I will lead you with light so bright that you will know for any particular moment you are on the right path."

9th May, 1993.

118 "I am your God you shall have no other. I am your light. You are wandering around in the darkness if you don't have Me.

Today My son I ask you to let people know that they are wandering around in the darkness and that I am the light. I am the light you need in your life."

10th May, 1993.

120 "Wherever you go you will find people who claim to be learned, be careful. Ask yourself: *Do they know Christ?* Keep always firm in your mind your goal to meet Me in Heaven. Ask yourself: *Does this person aspire to live the kind of life I'm trying to live?*

After you have answered these questions you will know what is in your midst. Quite often it will be practical atheism and apostasy."

11th May, 1993.

121 "Life is a series of challenges. Life is a series of days made up of joyful and sorrowful moments. It is necessary to add supernatural light to these happenings to see the glorious mysteries of God. I am your Father in Heaven, I will lead you through your life. I will be at your side when you are happy, when you are sad, I am there it is just a matter of you realising My presence.

Talk to Me, I am your friend. Tell Me how your work was today, or about how things are with your friends and family, tell Me about your dreams and ambitions, ask for all you need in all circumstances. Ask and you shall receive.

Bring Me into your life. Bring Me into every moment, every event. Acknowledge that I am there with you and you will be comforted by the fact that you are not alone. And you will have a force greater than any on earth with you."

11th May, 1993.

122 "Love is a beautiful thing. If you live My message of love, you too will be truly beautiful and people will be attracted to that beauty. It is then that you will have the opportunity to bring them closer to Me, to show them the source of all life and love.

The people who come into your life are all important and all need your encouragement and help either by prayer or a few gentle words. But when you speak about supernatural matters don't be like those who go on for hours. Be short. Say briefly and simply what it is the Spirit is prompting you to say, and no more.

It is essential that you work on finding the right time and the right place to share My message by words. But your actions and prayers ought to be continuous, no matter where you are or how harsh the environment. Remember, I am with you.

Those who share your love for Me, your Heavenly Father, sometimes need reminding of their duty to spread the faith. *Example is the best reminder.*

Love all. That person next to you on the train or in front of you on the footpath, that person has a soul. Pray, Pray then. Prayer My son, it's the answer. Prayer is what will unite the world as one in My Son Jesus Christ. The time is at hand, please do My work."

12th May, 1993.

123 "Try. This one word sums up all I ask of you. Just try, I am your God, I know all your weaknesses and limitations. I know you. When you work; when you play; in your friendships; in your prayer; in all you do; just try.

I will see when you conquer your weaknesses, I will see when you fall trying. When you fall trying, when you fail, when you fall to your weaknesses, I see. But I see that you wanted to love Me, but your wretched body didn't allow you to fully express your love. Try again, that's all I ask of you. It is when you are trying to love Me that you will be at your best. It is when you are trying to love Me that I turn your weaknesses into strength. It is when you are trying to love Me that I am there most, by your side, for you to lean on.

If you don't try, you won't find a way to Heaven. Those who had one talent and used it to it's fullest found Heaven. Those who had ten and used five didn't love Me, they loved the world.

You have been entrusted with many talents you must use them all. If you love Me you will not let them lay idle. To those who have been given a great deal, a great deal will be asked. You can only fail if you don't try."

12th May, 1993.

125 "There are leaders, and there are leaders. To accept a position of leadership is to accept responsibility. Responsibility for people. *However, modern day leaders and leaders throughout time have forgotten that each person has a soul and should be treated accordingly.*

Pope John Paul II is a beautiful man and by far the greatest leader this century. He radiates love through prayer and action. He has struggled endlessly with selfishness so as to become completely selfless, and give all that he has and is to Me (totus tuus), your Heavenly Father. He is My instrument, he does My work, he sows My seeds, he prunes My vine. He has truly fulfilled his role as Vicar of Christ.

Pray for him My son. Study him, read about him, look closely and you will find a man living an extraordinary high level of sanctity. I have given you the perfect example in My Son Jesus Christ, but if you are looking for an example, alive and near to you, of a Christ like person, look to Pope John Paul II.

Then act. See that he has followed My Son and that he has persevered in that following, then do the same yourself. I am your God, and I am with you."

13th May, 1993.

126 "The weather changes from sunshine to rain, but My love is constant and always there with you. Your health changes from good health to sickness, but My love is always there

with you.

(.....) Your physical illness will fade, your spiritual health will remain eternally, if you remain in My love.

This is why I tell you, even in times of physical illness remember the joy of knowing Me. Remember the joy of having Me in your heart. I don't abandon you in sickness, I am always with you.

Have faith and your illness will not be a burden. Your illness is all that you have to offer Me for your sanctification on some days."

14th May, 1993.

127 "Life is all important, the most wonderful gift I have ever given. The abuse or destruction of life is one of the greatest sins against Me, your Father in Heaven. *It is this that is the stone around the neck of the Western World that is drowning in the waters of self-indulgence, self-preservation, and comfort seeking.*

Abortion is only one part of it. Everybody in many ways everyday abuses the gift of life, the most common offence is laziness.

You were born to work. You were born to be saints and it is your work that will make you a saint. But until the day you die, you must stand firm in your belief that it is I, your God who gives life and therefore only I, your God, should take life.

Abortion is murder. *From the first moment of conception a human being is forming and a soul is present in the mother.* Don't compromise.

Murder is murder. Who has the right to say one life is more important than another.

Suicide is a sad product of the mixed messages throughout the world. New and old man-made messages designed to bring money and power into the hands of a few people.

Life is wonderful. I have sent My Son, Jesus Christ, that you may have life and have it to the fullest. Celebrate in your life and bring this message to all you meet."

14th May, 1993.

128 "May is Mary's month. The Mother of God. The most beautiful creature I ever created. In Mary you will find care and concern for even the smallest details. Mary is a mother, she knows what you need. You are her son, she loves you as she loved Jesus. When she wept for Jesus she also wept for you. She is, the *'Mother of the World'* and is greatly disturbed that her household has strayed.

But in any household there is one or two that keep the faith and in time bring the rest of the family back to My love. (.....) Bring her family, the world, back to your Heavenly Father's love, little by little.

She has revealed to others the way in which this should be done:prayer; the Mass; the Rosary; and, fasting. Her love is stronger than all the love and attention you have ever been shown put together.

All this love will come to you every moment of every day if you open yourself to her.

In this month of May, try especially in the area of devotion to Mary. (.....) Love, Love, Love is the answer.

Mary is your mother and she loves you dearly, consecrate yourself to her each day and the graces of her love will flow through your work, prayer and relationships."

15th May, 1993.

129 "You My son have a path to follow. You don't know where the path is going, that is one of the major parts of your faith journey. You must trust in Me your Heavenly Father to

guide you and show you the way. *I only enlighten you as to your direction one step at a time*. Just trust in Me and all will be well. You have nothing to fear, you have no right to fear. Your job is simply defined, but difficult. Your job is to follow.

All the best leaders in the world are not good worldly leaders because they go out on a limb on their own. They are good leaders because they are good followers. There is no need for you to be a leader. Be a follower, follow Me, and I will lead you to where it is you are destined to go.

All those around you will mistaken you for a great leader, but you and I will know that you are really a follower. Follow Me and Follow My Son Jesus Christ. Each day you must hunger for truth, justice, loyalty and love, and the many other wonderful virtues. You must hunger to be a virtuous man. You must hunger to be a saint, after all it is for this you were born. In everything you do you must hunger to follow My way with a song of joy, peace and love in your heart. Be humble, be a follower, be Mine."

15th May, 1993.

130 "There is a time and a place for those few words for that friend of yours. Find that time, find that place, then say or do what it is you ought.

Ask for the gift of fortitude and the Holy Spirit will fill you with the desire and the strength in each moment to do whatever it is you ought to do.

Timing is important, but timing can never be an excuse for cowardice. The time is right now for many things. The time is right now to love Me by giving Me this moment, by giving Me each moment, by doing what it is you ought to be doing when you ought to be doing it. Don't delay, don't be lazy, don't be a slob, Esto Vir(be a man) and then be a saint."
16th May, 1993.

131 "People are weak. You are weak. Why are you so surprised that this person does this or that wrong? Haven't you done many times worse yourself? And it was a bad example to the children, but haven't you been a bad example to children?

You cannot protect the children from everything, even though you love them very much. You must let them go. I am your God and I let you go, I give you freedom. You too should let them go, but don't close your eyes, and work all the harder to install good ideals and values in their minds.

They are bombarded everywhere they go, even in Catholic schools, with trash, with apostasy, with godless ideals and selfish testimonies from godless people. This is what you are up against.

You say: 'it is impossible that in the little time I spend with them that I should balance their scales with good to fight all this bad!' You are right, you are just one small man, it is impossible that you should.

But open your eyes. I am your God, your Father in Heaven, and I shall send the Spirit upon those you speak to and spend time with, and they will be touched by My love in you. On your own you can do nothing, united in My love there is nothing you cannot do."

16th May, 1993.

132 "Family. Family. Family. You must push and emphasise the importance of family. *If the family unit and family morals had not been broken down by Western Society the world would not be in the dark pit of sin which it is.*

The return of family importance and family values and morality are the secret to bringing the world out of this pit, the secret to the world finding the light, My Son Jesus Christ.

You must touch people by your deep concern for them,

especially your family, you must show them that they are precious and very important in your life. Other people may or may not see your love for your family, but they will not be able to help feel it by the way you live your life, doing the little things well.

Work endlessly and untiringly at this task of family. You tell Me that you encounter opposition to your love for Me (.....) and I tell you, wasn't it written that no prophet, no one that loves Me and keeps My Son's way, will be loved in his home town. Love them and their hearts will melt, and they will find Me.

Your family is important, even if you feel you are getting nowhere, don't be discouraged, be patient. You must be careful never to tire in loving them because one tired moment could cost you a month's work, if you are tired say nothing it is too dangerous.

Love all, but especially love your family, selflessly and you will bring My love to them without them even recognising it."

17th May, 1993.

133 "Of upmost importance is love for the Holy Trinity, Father, Son and Holy Spirit. You must know that I am in the Son and the Son is in Me. Together, Father, Son and Spirit are one God, three Persons. John in his gospel beautifully illustrates this many times and emphasises it.

To believe in the Trinity is very important, it is one of the principle truths of the Catholic faith. Take time, My son, often to reflect and meditate on this mystery.

Don't let your human limitations discourage your heart felt belief, remembering always, I am your God. You should not seek to understand this, just become more familiar with each Person of the Trinity by invoking each of us individually to help, guide, or guard you. By speaking to us about your ambitions, or weaknesses, or troubles.

We want to hear from you more and more. Our delight is in being with you, sons of man. So bring us into all your human activities.We will be there in constant conversation, an instant crowd you might say. But one who will be the best company."

17th May, 1993.

135 "It is the youth that must foster My love in their hearts, at these urgent times, for My message to be spread universally. You are called to live as the first Christians did. Looking out for each other, loving and caring selflessly for the community. Unite yourself with those you know who follow Christ, often; they will give you encouragement and strength to carry the cross at times when it seems more difficult. At times when you seem all alone.

This is one of the fruits you receive from the Mass. When you gather to celebrate the Mass you gather not as a series of individuals, but as a community. Community prayer is essential. Family prayer is beautiful. It may seem impossible to think that you would have your whole family kneeling in a circle praying. Nothing is impossible for Me your Heavenly Father and God.

Your youth is a beautiful gift, don't waste it, as it is temporal. Use your energy now to follow vigorously the plan I have for you. You must use all the human means available and then I will do the rest. You want for big things, that is good, I want for big things for you too My son, but I can only work on what you give Me. Work hard to give Me good foundations to work with. Pray hard that you should always know that I am with you. And suffer long and hard in My name. You have chosen to follow Christ and this is synonymous with suffering.

Call your young friends to join you. You must keep firm in

your mind the dangers of becoming attached to the things of this world. You must detach yourself from all that is worldly. In this I am saying you must love Me, the Lord, your God with your whole heart, your whole mind, your whole body and your whole soul. You must have no other god.

You cannot be attached to material things, otherwise they will become your god. Don't worry about money or it will become your god. Don't be so concerned at every moment about comfort or it will become your god.

Remember how Christ lived, He had nothing, but He never went without.

Go then and love all people in the name of the Father and of the Son and of the Holy Spirit."

18th May, 1993.

137 "Mary is your Mother and she loves you very dearly. Ask her to watch over you, to guide you, to assist you, and she will. She loves to help you especially in bringing you closer to Me your Heavenly Father. She wants to unite the whole world in My love. You must struggle in your love of Me and ask Mary to help you to always stick by this struggle.

You must bring your love for Mary to others. You must show them that Mary is part of the Heavenly Family and deserves their attention. But be patient in your apostolate, and be patient with those who don't understand your devotion to Mary.

During these end times Mary plays the greatest part in preserving the faith and building a cohort to continue to live in My love by prayer, the Mass, the Rosary, the Eucharist, Confession and sacrifice. You ask Me what it is I ask of you, this is what I ask: entrust yourself to your Mother's guidance and do these things constantly.

Mary is fruit. She is sweet and beautiful. She is full of love and compassion. Cry to her, she will hear you and answer your call.

You are living in a time often spoken about by false prophets, a time of change in the world. The evil one is running wild, but it will get worse, you will be able to see it as light as day. This time should not alarm or disturb you, it will get worse.

But faith My child, I am your Father and I will look after you. A time is coming when you will live united to Me, that is what you live for. Live for My love."

19th May, 1993.

138 "You are always in a hurry, slow down. Let's do things at My pace, to My plan. Let's just take one thing at a time and do it and do it well. Don't 'just do it', do it well. *Aim for perfection and at least you will do your best.* Then raise your eyes to Heaven and say, "Father this is my best, I offer it to you, please accept my lowly gift and by it help Me to grow in love of you." Then move on to the next task and do the same.

Repetition of this idea put into practise many times a day will lead to your sanctification.

Little by little, slowly you will learn what it is I want of you. There is no need to hurry, I have it all planned. I have a special plan just for you and this plan is much better than you could imagine, it is better than the best plan you could plan for yourself. It is not your job to plan but to pray, so that you can discover My plan for you, then act upon it."

19th May, 1993.

139 Jesus: "Today you must tell the world that time is short. Before long I will be with you again. Yes, my second coming

is at hand. You My brother, carry My cross and do My work, prepare My way. My mother has specially formed and selected Pope John Paul II for this time in the world. The evil one is not happy at this. The Pope is a great instrument of your Father in Heaven and in a single day, in a single address can return many hundreds, even thousands of hearts to a fuller love of Me. You must pray for the Pope, the death of the Pope before a natural death would be disastrous and there are some who are not as fond of the Pope as you.

In these times persecution will occur. Throughout time since I left the earth Christians have been persecuted, but it will become worse than ever. People will shed blood, people will lose their lives. Share My cross. No servant is greater than his master. I your Lord, Jesus Christ, suffered, as My servant how do you expect you will escape this suffering. But more than this, you must suffer lovingly. Do it for love and suffer acceptingly.

Many who are very close to Me don't understand these times. There are many manifestations of the Holy Spirit taking place to warn you, but due to the increasing level of apostasy in the world many of the faithful are not interested in these many warnings and won't be until the Church approves them. Their devotion and reliance on Rome is beautiful and brings Me much joy. (.....) If you are concerned, go to Mary your loving Mother. Mary is appearing to many and speaking to many more. She is appearing right here in Australia. If you are relying on people to believe you, I'm sorry, you will be sadly disappointed. You must seek refuge, in the Immaculate Heart of Mary, from the attack and pain that will come from non-believers.

On your own you are dust, but I have taken you and done great things for you, I have lead you through a conversion. Your love for Me has never been stronger or more complete, but be wary that you don't become lazy or lukewarm. I will vomit the lukewarm from My mouth. You must continue to pray, especially the Rosary, go to Mass daily, go to confession regularly (at least once a month), fast, and work on bringing your friends to a greater love of Me.

Above all trust. Do My will and all will be provided. You will have all you need and more. You will have peace and love."

20th May, 1993.

140 "Everyone has a vocation. It's a matter of time and patience. This time is needed to dig, to search before finding. Dig, dig. Dig deep into your heart, abandon everything to Me, just trust. As you dig disregard anything that attaches you to the world, discard anything that is selfish. All that you do must be done out of love, and love is selfless. So you must throw away anything that leads you to be selfish, or at least rectify your intention.

I have a plan for each and everyone of My sons and daughters and I have a plan for you. In you is a vocation, just be patient. Could I expect you to do My will without leading you and showing you the way. I will show you the way, but you must follow and stay close to Me so that you don't lose Me. Because if you lose Me, you lose the way. I will show you in subtle ways. Don't be anxious or concerned about the future. Do your best with the moment I provide you with now. *For now there is only one thing I want of you, love Me the Lord your God with your whole heart, mind, body and soul, by doing things well and by loving all those around you.*

When the time comes for you to make your next step, or for the path of your vocation to be further revealed to you, it will be. Trust."

20th May, 1993.

141 Jesus: "We are in a time of urgency, all around things are happening to promote the devil's reign. He asked for more power and time and it was given to him, but this will all come to an end. Just when the devil looks to be in charge all will change for the better, forever.

The heel of My Mother will crush the head of Satan and he will be returned and detained in hell forever."

God the Father: "You have nothing to fear My sons and daughters, each one of you must do your own little bit. It may seem insignificant, but little by little we will win. *Evil cannot reign over good, evil cannot victor over good, you must trust in Me and do as I ask courageously.*

These end times are times for saints. (.....) This is how it is, more than ever, there is a need for saints and martyrs. And it is important now that people begin thinking in these terms. To be a saint, it must be a goal that completely fills your heart and soul. No one will be a saint without consciously trying to better themselves and be a good person.

You are presently in the end times, the next ten years will be the most important since My Son Jesus walked on the earth, his second coming is at hand. Be ready. Those who were not ready were shut out of the party and not allowed to enter.

So I tell you be ready, follow My Son Jesus Christ. He will lead you to Me, the Father."

21st May, 1993.

142 Jesus: "You are always seeking to be noticed, to be seen, to be exalted for the wonderful things you do. Are you not forgetting something? You can do nothing without Me, but only by My grace. The glory belongs to Me. Be in the habit of saying, 'All glory and honour be to you Lord Jesus Christ.'"

God the Father: "You must be little, I am just waiting for you to empty yourself, to become little. Then I will fill you more than ever with My love, strength and grace and make you great. I have big plans for you My son but you must abandon your plans and lovingly accept and adopt Mine.

Hiddeness is the secret. You need more practise in working behind the scenes. You are very good at working in the spotlight. You must purify your intention in everything you do by remaining as hidden as is suitable for the given moment.

You must train yourself to listen to the Spirit's promptings so that you know when to speak up, when to act, when to walk in the spotlight and when to remain behind the scenes. Then you will know humility of intention. Then be humble, even if you are in the spotlight, be humble.

Beware false humility, if you are talented don't deny it foolishly. Accept the applause but remember it is by My grace that you do well. Remember who the glory and honour belongs to.

You must be little and humble."

21st May, 1993.

143 "Any act of violence cannot be an act of love. If you love you will not kill. My will has no violence contained in it, no aggression, but love.

War is wrong and violates many principles of Catholic faith. To take a life in any circumstances, especially war, is murder and a sin against Me. War breaks down morals and values, with compromise. *If you compromise on the Catholic principles of life, which are elementary, then there is no doubt any faith that remains will be weak and waiver in the wind.*

The two world wars of this century are very much responsible for the moral state of the world today. When on such a large scale you promote the destruction of human lives as being acceptable and even necessary then you must accept the dire consequences that will follow.

Leaders were, and continue to be, fools with regards the massive effects little things they do have on a society or a nation.

Humans think illogically often, you think always of justifying what you are doing. So war breaks out, people are killing people, so other people start behaving promiscuously, with the logic that it couldn't be as bad as killing someone. Or, if killing is all right, sex out of marriage is all right.

I want to cry out to those people, 'you are selfish.' But they won't listen. Cry out for Me, tell people. Learn that you yourself are selfish and then be selfless. People will think, this is strange, what's wrong with him. *Selflessness is normal, natural, and beautiful for a Christian.*

Do you see the effects of violence? Don't close your heart or harden your heart because all around you is violence. Soften your heart by My love and remember I am with you. Pray that others will have softer hearts. And spread My peace. I tell you this, before long violence and anger will be conquered by My love. You will see it happening in the people around you. My peace will reign on earth again before long. My peace will fill the hearts of people.

I have a plan, but be strong because before this, all those who are faithful to Me will undergo a rough period of persecution. This will be a period of pain, but fear not I am with you and will spare all those who love Me and bring them to live in My love forever."

22nd May, 1993.

144 "If it doesn't please Me why do it? *Are you serious about living the way I want you to live?* Then you must realise the importance of the cross.

When My Son walked on this earth He experienced opposition and pain, He was rejected, He died. You say you don't want to do this or that. Would you want to die on a cross? But you My son, you do want to, you just don't realise that you won't be happy until you learn to accept and love the cross.

The cross is hard and cold, like the world, but you can make yourself soft and warm by the cross. You ask Me for direction, follow the way of the cross. I'm not saying pick the hardest thing to do, I'm just saying that whatever you do you must bear the weight of the cross. Half hearted attempts at tasks are not good enough, you must work hard, you must face up completely to the task, not just absorb the enjoyable parts of different things you do.

Carry the cross everywhere you go. Don't be afraid, you can do it. You haven't been there before; go there. If you have something to do: do it. It is impossible you tell Me: good, so when you use everything available to you and it comes true you will know that it must have been Me who made it possible. Anything is possible for Me your Heavenly Father. Accept the pain of the cross. You say that you love Me, if you do you will carry My cross."

22nd May, 1993.

145 Mary: "(.....) I am your Mother, I hold you close to My heart always, I care for you and watch over you. You don't see Me but you should know I am there, never letting you out of My sight. (.....)"

22nd May, 1993.

147 "Convert. This is My plea to the world. Those who are away from the Church, come back. Those in a state of mortal sin, go to confession and sin no more. Those who are not

Catholic, convert.

Whatever your state in life, whatever your position on the spiritual journey, you need a conversion. Conversion is a continuous process of change, of new love.

If today you hear the words of Christ harden not your hearts, but convert. Be converted to a fuller love. Today start working on your hearts, ask My Son to help you work on your heart and form it into a heart full of love and compassion.

Convert and do not think that conversion is a trait of a fanatic. Lack of conversion is a sure sign of contentment and lukewarmness. You are called to change always, continuously. Don't compare your love for Me with someone else's, don't allow yourself to be tarnished by spiritual jealousy, only I can read men's hearts. *So if your heart is in the right place you have nothing to fear, for I your God judge by the heart, not by appearances and this is why men should never judge because they cannot read men's hearts.*

It is clear that you need a conversion today and another tomorrow. *Conversion is a renewal of love for Me which is preceded by a recognition of My love for you.* I love you, convert. Convert the world."

22nd May, 1993.

151 "(.....) You are sons and daughters of God, behave as such. Today I want to speak to you about unity of life. It is important that Catholics begin to be full on. It is important that Catholics begin to live truly Catholic lives with Christ at the centre of them. It is important that Catholics begin to live unity of life.

If you are a doctor, you are not a doctor and a Catholic, you are a Catholic doctor. Your profession and your religion are inseparable. You must live as Christ did, there was suffering and pain. He had to tell people the truth. He had to tell people they were doing things wrong that offend God. You are a doctor, but if it doesn't cost, if you are not persecuted at least rarely, then ask yourself are you a Catholic doctor, are you living your faith?

No matter what you do you must try to make My Son Jesus Christ, the centre of your activity. Ask yourself many times a day: What would Christ do now? And you will find yourself walking out, or speaking out for your faith, on many more occassions. Don't be scared, I give you the grace always to do what it is I am asking of you. The Holy Spirit will fill you with words and you will move into a greater love of Me. But it costs. Learn very early in the piece, that it costs to love Jesus and follow His way, but His way leads to Me, your Father in Heaven. Isn't that what you want.

I am with you My son."

25th May, 1993.

152 "You are doing fine. You must stay calm. At no stage of My plan is there a time when you should lose your calm, your serenity. You must remain in My love and you must remain close to Me always, so that you can be aware of My will.

The 'will of God' many will say, and laugh. They will ask you, how do you know the will of God. And you will say, 'He speaks to me,' and they, 'that's impossible.' Remember always nothing is impossible for God, nothing. You must trust always in My will and never lose faith.

Faith is what sustains joy. And your joy is a gift from Me your Heavenly Father. I give you joy as a taste of life everlasting, of the life to come and to earn this life you must struggle endlessly as a human being to seek out and do My will. Those who laugh at this as a goal are the unfortunate creatures who have fallen victim to the western world's apostasy.

Remember your job is to do My will and do it with joy."

25th May, 1993.

153 "Love My son. Love My way, love My will. I love you child, I will help and protect you, but don't think that this means no harm will come to you. You must suffer as My Son Jesus Christ suffered.

The secret is love. Today tell all your brothers and sisters to work on building hearts that can really love. Love costs, and love of Me your Heavenly Father costs a great deal, especially at the present time in the world. Selflessly you must all approach the world. Selflessly you must approach your lives and your daily activities.

We all have one ambition: Christ will reign. First then let him reign in your hearts, then your mind, body and soul. Christ will reign, its only a matter of time and as I have told you, time is short. Each and everyone of My children has a mission, please abide.

Live in My love instead of holding back little things for yourself, give everything so that I can then return to you abundantly. I will give you many, many gifts, unexpected gifts. My plan for each of My children is beautiful. Does a father on the earth plan good and beautiful things for his children? Well won't My plan from Heaven be of much greater beauty? Pray and you will know the next step to make.

To all My children I say, don't hold back, give selflessly and you will find true joy and true happiness. You will taste eternal life, you will live in My love and then you will know how to love."

26th May, 1993.

154 "Fight. Fight My son against those inclinations that lead you to be easy and weak on yourself, or to neglect your duties. Your body was entrusted to you for many good reasons, but one of them was not that it might be your master. You must be master of your body, you must push it a little further when it says, 'enough.'

The body always says 'enough' with plenty in reserve. Tell Me, if you were to go through the passion of Jesus freely, where would your body have said, 'enough'. Your body is weak, but you can make it strong by disciplining the body.

You are having trouble fasting, think of the positive. To see you putting yourself through the suffering of fasting brings Me great joy, so think of Me and the joy you bring Me, by your act of love.

Many around you will say, 'it's not necessary to get to Heaven', and they are right. But it helps, and it helps in many ways and this is because it not only helps you to get to Heaven, but fasting helps those souls on earth who need help and it also greatly helps souls in purgatory. *Fasting saves souls.*

Go out and tell the world to fast, twice a week: Wednesday and Friday. Yes, your Mother has spread this message before, but the message is the same for Australia and you must spread it.

Fasting adds strength to everything you do, and fasting will be a large contribution to seeing Christ reign on earth again."

26th May, 1993.

155 "Today My son pray. Pray unceasingly. This is not to mean that you leave the world and find a cave. No, in everything you do, speak to Me throughout. Tell Me how it's going, what the difficulties are with the task, and tell Me the joys involved. Remember My son to pray is to build our friendship, I invite you to absorb My love through ordinary

daily activities.

Prayer is beautiful and powerful. If you knew just how powerful prayer was you would never say a Rosary without thinking about the words, you would never lose your attention in Mass. *Prayer like fasting saves souls.*

Save souls, isn't that a beautiful task. Go out today and tell the world to pray and fast in order to save souls.

It is important that you pray, because I am your Father in Heaven and I await you to join Me so we can be one in a fuller sense, and if I do not know you, if you do not pray, you shall not enter. Only those who hear the Word and do the will of your Heavenly Father shall enter.

One of the most important parts of your prayer is to read My Word. *Anyone claiming to follow Christ who doesn't read My Word daily are kidding themselves.* My Word provides food for your souls just as the Eucharist does, only in a smaller way.

These words have been food for your soul and look how your life has changed, but you couldn't appreciate the Eucharist and My Word as you have since I spoke to you. My son, blessed are those who live Holy Mass and do My will by listening to My Word, their's is the kingdom of Heaven. Yes, they shall surely enter and be immersed in My love for eternity.

I know you cannot understand what that means, or what that would be like. Be patient My son, and love Me, and do My will, and you shall taste Heaven yourself.

I long to be with you My child. Why cannot you humans see, that I am your God and My delight is in being with you and speaking with you?

Detach yourselves from the world, fools, and pray."

27th May, 1993.

156 "The angels are fighting a war. My angels are strong and always will be, but if you don't believe in them and show them that you do by correspondence of a supernatural nature with them, then you cut yourself off from a great deal of help from Me your Father.

I use angels as a vehicle for many graces which I supply for you to struggle with your daily trials, but all too often these graces go unused or are 'returned to sender' because of lack of belief in angels.

My angel will go before you and prepare your way if you ask him too. Ask him to guard you from your enemies and he will.

During these times, of great persecution of hard line Catholics, you must trust more and more in Me your Father and the work My angels do. They will find a spot in people's hearts and they will win over that spot and from there they will move, fighting and winning more and more of that persons heart until finally that person will cry, 'Why do I fight your will Father, I give Myself to you now: All that I am is yours.'

Angels work on hearts to save souls here on earth. Prayer gets souls out of purgatory.

Your guardian angel is more beautiful and caring, and watchful than anyone you know on earth. He will guide and guard you. Thank him for that, and thank Me for him. You must start to appreciate the many gifts I have given you to fight My war, and a war it is.

This is a war for souls. There are no guns or knives. Just angels, and devils and souls. Join the angels in the fight to win Me souls for Heaven.

Prayer will win this war. Prayer and loving action."

27th May, 1993.

157 " (.....) The world is in great danger but it doesn't realise. The media is constantly promoting the wrong things, this will be difficult to change, but pray that it does. The devil is very strong in the media, even in what appears to be good, be careful. The devil is cunning and he uses 90% truth to get his 10% of lies across, and he does it in such a way that 10% grows of its own, because it undermines the 90% truth and legitimises more wrong."

28th May, 1993.

158 "Women are important, very important in My plan. It was once said that if you corrupt men, you have corrupted men. But if you corrupt women you have corrupted society. This is what has happened and this is My message to women young and old:

Demand what is good and proper and pleasing to God. Demand respect, in particular for your bodies. Dress modestly and properly remembering that men are not made of steel, but flesh and blood and they are affected by the way you dress, act, and move, so be careful. Be prudent.

I want the world to be a clean, loving place. Mary is the *'Mother of Purity'* and the Mother of all women young and old. Ask her to teach you Holy Purity, follow her example of chastity, live in love not in the selfish indulgences of the flesh. Act out of love purely and cleanly and you will change the world. From the beginning of time men have largely been responsible for the corruption of society, women will be largely responsible for the return of good, clean Catholic principles. Demand what is good, clean and proper. Demand what is pleasing to God."

28th May, 1993.

161 "Little things are beautiful, big things are necessary. Of you My son I ask both, but above all I ask that you let My Spirit guide you so that you know always what I am calling you to do. If you want to have confidence in what you are doing you must learn to know the Holy Spirit. He is the Sanctifier. He is the one who will guide you along your path of My will. The Holy Spirit is the friend who cares and inspires, who motivates those who feel that the forces are against them.

The love of the Father is the greatest power, a force greater than any on earth. The Holy Spirit is full of gifts. You should ask that you be well endowed with these gifts. And you should thank the Holy Spirit when you see that you have received abundantly in these things. Ask and you shall receive.

You are sons and daughters of God. Your heart is absorbed in the goal of doing God's will for the end, 'sanctity', because you know this is the only way to love Me, your God.

The Holy Spirit will lead you, but you must want to be led by the Holy Spirit, you must want to be a man of God, you must want to be a servant of God. Say to yourself often: I will serve! And I your God, knowing that in you I have a loyal instrument will send the Paraclete to give you strength in your service of all men and women. I will show you love."

29th May, 1993.

162 "Sin is to walk away from Me, to abandon Me. Nobody wants to be abandoned. Think of it like this: What if I were to abandon you? What if I were to leave you? You would not be. Now do you understand that I am with you always? Because if I was not with you, you would not be.

Repent today, I do not condemn you but invite you to life. Repent, be baptised, go to confession and sin no more. For I am the Lord your God who loves you dearly, and he that believes and does as I say will live with Me and in Me. Yes, he will live in My love. And how comforted you are by the world, by the love of the world, but forever is a long time. Isn't that human, earthly, worldly love shortlived and incomplete? Don't you hunger for more? Yes. That love lacks Me. I will bring completeness to your earthly life, only I, not money or goods, or people, I your God.

Today abandon sin, not I your God. See that I am life, I am the living water that feeds the souls of all who thirst for more, for all who thirst for love, for all who thirst for Me, for all those who thirst for eternal life and eternal love in Me.

Your life on earth is a short stay, a preparation for the next life, don't be foolish and proud. Admit your littleness, your weaknesses, your wretchedness and repent, and return to My love everyday. And in My divine mercy I will give to you gifts more abundantly than you ever imagined. You shall live. Where on earth do you do wrong, own up to it, and get presented with a gift? Where on earth? Do you not see, only the love of a father would judge as such for his son. I am your Father, you are My son, I love you, do My work."

29th May, 1993.

163 " (.....) Young people are searching in all the wrong places, they don't realise that I am the Way, the Truth and the Life. They comfort themselves in selfishness and pleasure in every moment possible but never realise that this is shortlived. Could it be that in their foolishness they think one day they will find sustained pleasure? That is what they are looking for but they are looking for it in the wrong places. In Me all will find life, sustained pleasure, eternal joy. But what of this earthly pleasure, it is temporary. When will they come to Me?

They will come to Me when they know about Me and My

Son and My Spirit, (.....) You see My son, it is your job to teach the world about Me. Because you don't fall in love with someone on the other end of the world you've never met. We'll if they don't know Me, how can they love Me. Bring them to know Me through the Rosary and through your writings and My words. If they knew Me, really knew Me, they would love Me."

30th May, 1993.

164 "You are surrounded by bad example, the secret is, don't compromise. *Don't compromise your love for Me.* If you love someone you do everything, even the smallest thing, for that person well, very well. It should be the same with Me. If you love Me you will love Me down to the last letter of My will. Even if that means giving your life for Me.

This is what love is all about. I sent My Son Jesus into the world to teach you about love and love My children is about carrying the cross. You can't fall in and out of love many times a day, but you can let your selfishness be a barrier to love.

Love is selfless and love is accepting the cross. This is what Jesus did and this is what each and everyone of you must do. You must love, but you must love the cross. If you don't love the cross, your love for Me is shallow and perhaps even self indulging. So often this is all human love is.

Carry the cross, suffer to save souls and then My friends you will know love, you will know the love of knowing God has found a home in you. You will know the unshakeable joy that this brings. And your life will take on a whole new direction. Do not be afraid, I am with you."

30th May, 1993.

165 "Why do you hesitate when you hear the promptings of the Spirit. You ask for the gifts of the Spirit and then you hesitate to act. Today My children you must learn to be docile.

Docility is beautiful, it is not stupidity, unless you look at it from an earthly perspective, but no, look at it from a supernatural point of view, which is so very natural to human beings.

To be docile to the promptings of the Spirit is to abandon yourself to the will of your Heavenly Father, to abandon your plans and ambitions and to adopt *the one holy and catholic ambition and goal: to do God's will.* To do as He asks, to do as the Spirit prompts you to do in each moment of the day. To live and abide by His word, to let His word find a home in your heart. To invite the good Lord aboard your ship as Master.

Today you must abandon yourself to Me your God, you must invite My Son aboard your ship as Master. And you must learn to live and love My word.

You feel helpless because you have not yet welcomed the Spirit. This is what the second Pentecost is all about. Each person individually must welcome the Holy Spirit into their lives.

You are living in changing times. Don't be alarmed by change."

31st May, 1993.

166 "Wake up fools. Do you not see that what is before you is all temporary, but what I offer is eternal, eternal joy and happiness. You don't even know what this means, but no eye has seen, nor ear has heard anything as beautiful as Heaven.

Tonight I would like to tell you about Heaven so that you spend time everyday thinking about Heaven, and this will give you strength to struggle and carry the cross.

You know when you do something right, and you know you have done what is good and proper, how you feel joy and peace in your heart, mind and soul. Well you feel this for a moment.

Well, Heaven is like that constantly. Because that joy is you finding Me your God living in you, and through your actions we are united or separated. Well, that feeling you get is very diluted. Heaven is complete union. On earth you are not able to experience the complete joy of Heaven even for a moment.

Consider times when you have abandoned everything to Me, out of loving trust, and then just rested in the love of My presence for a few moments. Well that is only a shadow of My love, and only a shadow of the love I want to share with you in Heaven.

Come My son, be led along the path of pain, suffering, and persecution and keep always firm in your mind your resolution to purify your intentions and act from the heart out of love. And that way none of your sufferings will go to waste and you will receive a high place in Heaven.

Heaven, My children is a reality. Live in hope, supernatural hope of My love and Heaven which are one in the same."

31st May, 1993.

167 Mary: "My child come now and rest in My love. The day is done and you have done your best, tomorrow you will try again to live out the will of God. All I did everyday on earth was this and this is your task. Try always to keep presence of God. He is there with you through it all. Like the best of friends My Son will not leave you and nor will I. I am your Mother and I am here to care for you. Come now and rest in My love."

31st May, 1993.

168 "You must work on changing your heart. For so long it has belonged to the world and now you want to give it to Me. Well you must work continuously now everyday on changing, so that it can be soft and gentle, but firm. Because what is in a man's heart is what a man speaks of. So discard anything in your heart that belongs to the world or is not pleasing to Me, your Heavenly Father. You must keep your heart free from attachments to the world, and give your heart to Me.

Each day hold it up to Me, lift up your hearts to the Lord, and I will help you work on your hearts, I will help you to form your heart just like Mine, and to do this you need one instrument, the cross.

The cross is what gives Christian hearts firmness. Firmness to remain in My love at times of trial, when it costs, the firmness required to be selfless.

Today if you hear the words of God, harden not your hearts. Pray My son that your heart be sufficiently softened so that you can love everything that happens in your life, every person that enters your life, and then you will follow My way. Then people will see your soft and gentle, but firm, heart and will say, 'Christ is passing by.' Yes, they will feel the presence of Christ My Son in your heart and their hearts will be softened also. This is My plan, to melt hearts, to soften them and then make them firm.

Today My children work on your hearts. Soften them and let My word in and make them firm by living My word and carrying My cross."

1st June, 1993.

169 "The way, the time, the place, your spirit, are all taken care of. You must focus on loving Me your God in every moment of the day. No matter what you are doing, your job is to love Me. Singleness of task. This is your job and this will

never change, you will always have only one job: give glory and honour to Me your God by loving Me with your whole heart, mind, body and soul.

Give Me your heart and I will make it gentle and kind. Give Me your mind and I will make it strong and wise. Give Me your body and I will make it a useful instrument. And give Me your soul and I will make it My home.

I want to live in you. One of the things that hurts the devil so much and one of the reasons why he wants to drag you away from Me in sin, is because I want to live with and in you. My delight is in being with you sons of men. So love Me and I will love you and together we will defeat the devil.

But be careful not to be proud, pride stunts your growth it dosen't allow you to love as My Son Jesus loved. You begin to judge and calculate and plan. *Pride is the enemy of trust.* You must trust Me My son, I am your Father."

1st June, 1993.

171 "You are fast to react to other people's failings and flaws, but slow to investigate your own. Today I call you to look at yourself. Take off your sunglasses of pride and open up and examine yourself honestly, make one firm resolution and then go off again and put it into practise.

This is the secret to conquering pride, you must often cut out the cancer of pride, especially if it rises up in your interior life. *Pride separates God from man.* The first sin of man was a sin of pride, not anything else. Eve thought she was greater than she was. So often you humans think you can be greater, this is the devil tempting you. You are little. You find your greatness in Me.

My greatness shines through men to give them the appearance of being great."
2nd June, 1993.

172 "My love is consistent and never failing. It's always there for you to reside in, or retire to if you feel the need. Keep good presence of God, keep Me always there in every little activity and My love will be like the sun on the plants and before long you will bloom.

Remember, I am the Divine Gardener and I have great plans for each part of My garden. Each part has My particular attention and each part will have a great harvest before My second coming. I am coming and I hold the keys of salvation.

All those who follow My Son Jesus Christ's example, hear My words and do My will, they shall be saved. But there will be many who ignore the warnings and they will never see the Kingdom of Heaven. My children now more than ever you are called to detach yourselves from the world, but never confuse this with leaving the world.

Your job is right in the middle of the world. You must do normal things, like normal people, but you must bring to every task a supernatural outlook. You must bring to every task and every person, My love.

My love. If you show them My love they will fall in love with it and want it for themselves. If you show them My love, they will want to be around you all the time.

Today, go out into the middle of the world with My love, they will see and desire this love and then you can show them My way.

You must be cheerful, because holiness and cheerfulness are synonymous. Do you expect to attract people to Christ if you are always unhappy?"

3rd June, 1993.

173 "It is not enough to just pray. You must work, and you must work harder than anyone you know.

It is like this you see: you want to be a man of God and do

My will, well there are many out there who are working against Me whether it be willingly or out of ignorance, but none the less they are working hard, very hard. They are selfish and they have no vision, but in the moment at hand they work hard to fulfil their selfish ambitions.

But fear not if you work as hard as they do, at My work, you will be three times more productive and infinitely more fruitful, *for the fruits of work are not in this life.*

Children of Mine, hear My call, work is important. Spread yourselves among the many professions and carry My cross and together we will link up, gather the huge harvest at hand and change the world.

Remain in the world My children, don't run away. Do what you are doing well, very well. If you can be the best, you have no excuse for not being the best. And those who are the best in their fields without Christ in their lives are only a fraction of what they could be if they had the flame of Christ in their hearts.

Those who do an honest day's work, they will have a place in Heaven. Those who are lazy and misuse their time, which is a gift from God, they have not quenched the living waters.

If you are like this My son make firm resolution to change. Each hour ask yourself: Is this hour a suitable gift to God? Then try harder in the next hour to please Me. I am always with you, but I have a particular closeness to hard workers."

3rd June, 1993.

174 "Today you must learn to live with Me each moment. *One at a time you and I will tackle the moments that make up the day.* We are a team. If you feel like it is becoming too difficult you must have lost Me or your trust in Me. If I am with you who could be against you.

I am the strength in our team, but you are the instrument.

You must fine tune the instrument to prepare it more and more. You must pray more, you must read more and you must spend more time with people. People are precious and important to My plan.

You must learn more about yourself and about people. You must learn how to deal with people so that they are alerted to the peace and calm you have in your soul. You must bring people My love. If you love them with My love, true love, selfless love, then they will soon hunger for Me.

Conversion can be a fast or a slow process. You as the instrument must do the work that I administer and no more. Be patient, souls take their time sometimes, but when they come around their love is overflowing, their devotion unending, and consistent and from their hearts.

Every person is different and precious. Until you start to treat them like this you will never be able to do My work effectively."

4th June, 1993.

175 Mary: "(.....) Pray now. Pray with your heart and all will be well. The secret to praying with your heart is putting yourself in the presence of God, acknowledging that Father, Son and Holy Spirit are here with you, along with all the saints, especially St. Joseph, your guardian angel and myself.

Then when you firmly believe that we are here with you, your heart will rejoice and that is prayer from the heart.

It is very natural for the human heart to be in a state of rejoicing. This is the day the Lord has made let us rejoice and be glad. Regardless of what is happening around you, your heart should be in the state of rejoicement, because it is united with God, it is a home for God."

4th June, 1993.

176 "Quite clearly you are attracted to My love My son. You see it is like this, although you must give a lot, you are given so much more, I will never be outdone with generosity. Those who give for Me, I in turn will give to them many times more. This is not to say that you should give only because you will receive more in return, like a good investment.

No, you must give out of love for Me and love for Me in your neighbour. Empty yourself out, give it all up. Give away those selfish appetites, fight them continuously and never think that the fight is won. When you rest in your eternal abode in My love, then the fight is won.

The devil never gives up, you must renew this emptying of yourself everyday. It's more than surrendering yourself, it's denying yourself out of love, it's dying unto yourself so that you can live in My love.

Love costs, the price: the cross. My Son, Jesus Christ, experienced the total giving up of His body in reparation for your individual sins. *Is it too much to deny your body constantly of the luxuries that make your body lazy and prevent it from being a good instrument of My work?*

If you are to be an instrument of My work you must first master your body and having done that you must renew this mastery in each moment of the day. There are many little battles in this war.

To win you must first take control of your own territory. Then keep control of it."

4th June, 1993.

177 "It is true that I the Lord your God will return to reign in glory on earth. This time is near at hand, but first you and all of mankind must suffer these end times.

Satan is running wild in the world, he has many followers working for him, but the sad thing is most of them don't realise they are doing his work. Be very careful of what worldly activities you involve yourselves.

The media is full of Satan's work but you must keep in touch with what is happening in the world. Read the newspaper, don't dwell on it, just skim over the main stories. This is much better than television news. *Don't watch television, all stations are Satan's stations*. He has infiltrated television perfectly and television is his main weapon, his most powerful instrument. (.....), *television is the thief of love*, and think about it: What does Satan dislike most? Love. Does it not all seem logical that he should use the power of continuous images in every household to try and win.

Remain always firm in your belief in Me, I am the Lord your God. I shall reign on earth before long. You must guard yourself against what the world calls entertainment. *Parties have become an oasis of sin for Satan*. Many souls are lost at parties to sex, drugs and alcohol.

Why? Because it feels good. You must learn that while you can do many things, this does not mean you should do them all.

Respect your bodies, I your God have given them to you for eternity. When you come to be with Me in Heaven, at the end of the world you will receive your bodies back to be united body and soul again. Look after your bodies.

Above all pray more, avoid fruitless exercises that the world provides 24 hours a day. The world wants you to do many things but don't. Live truly Catholic, Christ-like lives, carry the cross and you shall see Heaven.

I am the Lord your God, I love you more than you could ever know. Live for Me in My love. Gather My sheep even if it means showing them these words of warning.

These times belong to Satan, you must keep My word alive. Satan has much charge over the world, you must change it. (.....) "

5th June, 1993.

178 "You must serve. Be servant to all. If someone asks something of you, as long as it doesn't take you away from Me, do it joyfully and well. Serve all people because I am in all people and just as I have washed your feet, you must wash each other's feet.

To follow My Son Jesus is to serve and to serve is to put yourself last. First should come all those around you. If a master is out and he returns tired and hungry, does he ask the servant to feed himself first and then bring his master's meal? No, the master eats first and the servant last.

Last is your position. Take the last place in the line and then you will learn to be little, you will learn to be a good and faithful servant. And to the good and faithful servant I shall entrust large matters but first you must prove yourself in small matters.

To read on your tombstone, "He lived his life in the service of Christ and all men". This is how I want you to live your life, so that, for the little it is worth, men shall think and say such kind words about you.

Forget yourself now and serve. Service is what all men were made for. Your work should be a service to society. By your work you should serve society and Me your God.

Love, as I have often told you, is all you need. If you love Me you will have everything physically, spiritually and materially that you need.

Serve, because those who serve are selfless. There is nothing in serving for self. Give yourself up to the service of man now and remember, when you serve the least of My brothers, you are serving Me."

5th June, 1993.

179 "The mini-judgement is a reality. People no longer realise that they offend Me. Out of My infinite Mercy I will provide a mini-judgement. It will be painful, very painful, but short. You will see your sins, you will see how much you offend Me everyday.

I know that you think this sounds like a very good thing, but unfortunately even this won't bring the whole world into My love. Some people will turn even further away from Me, they will be proud and stubborn. Satan is working hard against Me.

Poor souls, all of you, robbed of the knowledge of My love. Be ready for this judgement of Mine. Judgement is the best word you humans have to describe it, but it will be more like this: you will see your own personal darkness contrasted against the pure light of My love.

Those who repent will be given an unquenchable thirst for this light. Their love for Me then will be so strong that united with Mary's Immaculate Heart and the Sacred Heart of Jesus the head of Satan shall be crushed and he will be detained in hell forever. All those who love Me will join to help form the heel that crushes Satan.

Then as you all die naturally, your thirst for this light will be quenched, you shall see Me your God. You shall live in My love, you will be in Heaven.

Now do you see how important these times are? Don't wait for this mini-judgement, you must start to look at yourselves more closely so that you can see your faults and repent. You are fortunate to have the faith needed to read, believe and accept this message, you must not go away indifferent to it. You must examine yourself more everyday and pray in reparation.

All of you, be like the blind man. Each day you should cry, "Lord, open My eyes", and My Son will open your eyes so that you can see your wretchedness and repent.

Pray now more than ever and remember the world's standards are a false indication of My Justice. I am your God and while I am perfectly merciful to those who repent, I am perfectly just to those who do not.

Many people think that I your God won't mind, it's only little, they say. But it's not a matter of minding. I want people to love Me. Love respects little things as well as the big things and in the most case these little things are not so little.

Do not judge your actions, or other's actions, you are unable to judge, you are incapable of judging because you cannot read a man's heart.

You must love Me with your whole heart, with your whole mind, with your whole soul and with your whole strength.

Today is the day, do your best to renounce yourself and let Christ reign in your lives. You will never be ready for the mini-judgement, but some will be more prepared than others. You must aim to be one of those and bring as many others as you can to be prepared, or as prepared as possible.

Above all do not fear, I don't tell you all this to become scared. No, simply try to become better people each day, more than this I could not ask. I am your God, I am perfectly just and perfectly merciful. You are sons and daughters of Mine, does not a father look after his children? I send this message to spare you from any pain I can, but the pain that you experience by seeing the darkness of your soul is an act of love on My behalf. Do you not see that this will return many, many souls to a fuller love of Me. This will save many souls from the fires of hell.

This is the most important of all My messages: I am the Lord your God, you are My sons and daughters whom I love very much and My greatest delight is in being with you, and I want to be with you for eternity. Anything I do is done out of love for you My children. Trust in Me your Heavenly Father."

5th June, 1993.

180 "You say you love Me. This is easy to say, you could even get into the habit of saying this without thinking about what you are saying.

Today my children, let Me teach you about love. Love is something very holy. Love is Me, your God.

So to relate love, which I am, into a worldly context means to bring Me into your thoughts and actions.

I am God, I am Goodness, I am Perfection, I am Love. The world's idea of love is not love, it is selfish. People are selfishly using other people as stepping stones for their own fulfilment. But, this kind of behaviour only ever brings: hurt; anger; frustration; and emptiness.

Love My children is very different. Love is patient and kind. Love is selfless and doesn't keep a record of wrong. Love is eternal.

So often people say that they love each other, and then weeks later they hate the person. Be careful in your use of the word love.

Love on earth is two people united with Me. This is to say, people experiencing love don't need to sleep together, but rather, any two people spending time together, in person or by correspondence, who acknowledge Me the Lord your God and My presence, these two people are experiencing love. Love is to be united with Me your God. You cannot experience love if I am not present. I am love.

Sex is not love. Sex is selfish. Never confuse sex with making love. When two people male and female join in the physical act of intercourse and they acknowledge Me as Creator, and they are aware of the important role they have been entrusted with in the creation of man, then these two people are making love.

Furthermore, any artificial intervention to stand in the way of My creative powers, I have entrusted to humans, reduces the act to a mere animal act, sex.

All of you must rediscover the true meaning of love, you must learn to live in love. In Me, through Me and with Me, you find love. Where you take Me you take love.

Today My children bring Me to all places and to all people, bring Me into the world. Let the world rediscover real love. Let them be removed from their deprived state and enter into My love, which lasts eternally.

My children I love you, come now and experience My love through the sacraments and prayer and thus you will be able to experience love in the worldly context. *Unless a man or woman knows Me, through prayer and the sacraments, he or she does not know love.*

Here is My invitation, an invitation to love, please respond."

6th June, 1993.

182 "Waste no time, I am calling you to love Me completely in everything you do, right now. Don't say, 'When this is over I'll devote myself to God.' I am waiting here now, calling you to give yourself to Me now, completely, once and for all.

Say it, 'All that I am is yours Lord. For me I want nothing, all glory and honour be to you Lord Jesus Christ. You must increase Lord and I must decrease, so that it is no longer I that live but you that live in Me.'

Until each and everyone of you, My children, can say this

from your heart and try each day to live it, you will not know the fullest measure of My love on earth, which is a foretaste of Heaven, but only in the tiniest degree. It is only by surrendering yourselves to My love, abandoning yourselves to My trusting care, that you begin to live.

Join the Holy Father in saying, "Totus Tuus."

6th June, 1993.

183 "Look around you My people. Look at what you see: poverty; disease; robbery; immorality; you see a godless people. Australia is quite possibly the wealthiest country when it comes to natural and human resources, but you are trying to mix it with the best in the wrong areas.

Quite simply Australians need to go back to living simple lives not caught up in the materialism of these times.

Today My children you must learn to have only what you need. There are many people who have nothing, this is wrong when people are spending hundreds of dollars on shoes and hundreds of thousands of dollars on cars. You all must learn to give and share. There is plenty for everyone. My kind of plenty, not the world's kind of plenty. Because for the world's desire there will never be enough.

You all must realise that really you need so little to survive, and once you have My love sown in your hearts you will see that everything comes to those who trust in Me, your God.

I am the provider for the family. Never concern yourself or lose your peace of mind and heart because of financial matters. Ask yourselves every time you purchase do you need it. If you don't need it, put it back and put your money to better use.

The world is working on creating needs in people, making people feel that they need to have the best quality in everything, or the best brand, or the most. Don't be caught up in the chase for material possessions, because you can never win. And if you are caught up in it then you will never have enough, you will always want more, your quench will never be satisfied.

Come to Me My children and live in My love and I will give you rest, and quench your thirst and allow you to enjoy the little that you have. Those who chase material possessions rarely know how to enjoy them.

Money is a means of eating, being clothed and having shelter. Now is the time to realise that if you work hard and trust in God you will always have what you 'need.' For I am your Heavenly Father and I want all My children to be fed with the food of salvation, the precious body and blood of My Son Jesus Christ, clothed with the dress of eternity and sheltered in My home: Heaven.

Put your whole heart into loving Me and you will never be hungry. I am the Lord your God can you not see the selfishness and pointlessness of the material possessions race, no one comes to Heaven who is attached to the world. If you belong to the world, you cannot belong to Heaven. I am the Good Shepherd, I know My sheep and My sheep know Me. Where I go they follow.

My children, I was born into poverty in that stable, I never had anything except a garment and sandals, I trusted in My Father in Heaven and He always supplied for Me what I needed.

All you need is spiritual zeal, a heart that longs for Me and tries to please Me will never go hungry, My love is enough to keep men alive for years.

I am the Lord your God, do not place your trust and security in things of this world. Place your trust in Me, I am the only one worthy of it. Trust My children, I am your loving Father."

7th June, 1993.

184 Jesus: "It is not enough to say you love Me. He shall enter who listens to My word and does My Father's will."

God the Father: "Today you must live as Christians, bring your faith into everything you do. Today you must spread My faith not by fancy words, but by the way you act. Not just so your actions can be seen like the Pharisees. Today you must live out My word. From your heart shall come your actions. So if you make your heart the home of My word then you will do My will and the people around you will see your good works and praise Me your Father in Heaven.

I am what you are looking for, search no longer, but rest in My love. No longer should you fear or be anxious, for now that you rest in Me, all is taken care of.

Worry is a disease that has infected the world. Worry is a tool of Satan and attacks the beautiful virtue of hope. Have hope My children, the best you can hope for is Heaven. Be always in the state of grace and then if death, the worst human incident by the world's standards should come upon you, you will find Heaven. You will be united with Me your Heavenly Father. If you are in the state of grace, even death will not worry you.

Worry is useless. By worrying you offend Me in many ways. You deny that divine providence exists. You deny that Heaven exists above anything that is temporal. And you deny the gift of hope I have given to each of My children.

Does a child worry about where the money for the electricity bill will come from? No, the father does. Let Me take your cares from you, let Me be the one that takes care of all your needs. Abandon yourself to My love and you will see that I am your Father in whom you can place all your trust.

If you trust in Me you will not have a worry in the world. Your soul will be at peace. You will experience that joy that comes from union with me, you will experience that peace of heart, mind, and soul, that only comes from complete abandonment to Me. The days are long for those who carry the weights the world places on your shoulders. Come to Me your Heavenly Father and I will give you rest My children."

7th June, 1993.

186 "Tell all My children to return to the sacraments. They are your life. Without them you starve the soul of the necessary grace. Tell them to return to My love via the sacraments and prayer.

Go to confession My children, it is so important. Christ, My Son, said to the apostles, 'Whatever sins you forgive are forgiven and whatever sins you hold bound are held bound in Heaven.' *My children if you don't go to confession you tie My hands with the perfection of My justice, but more than this you deny yourselves of one of the greatest gifts I have given you through My Son.*

The grace you receive from confession is abundant, you should go regularly, even every week if possible, not only to confess mortal sins, but venial sins. Confess and you will have the strength from grace to carry on.

Then go to the Eucharist, receive My Son's precious body and blood worthily. At many, many Masses, large numbers of people are receiving My Son's precious body and blood unworthily, they have mortal sins on their souls, I am no longer living in them, they are not in the state of grace.

These two sacraments are vital if you are going to struggle along My way in the world today. If you are going to carry the cross you need strength, you need Me for I am strength, I am your all. Use the sacraments My children, they are precious gifts that are being misused and unappreciated.

Realise that I am your God, you are nothing of your own. I gave you the sacraments as a means of growing closer to Me and remaining in union with Me. Don't be foolish and proud, use the sacraments.

Times are near when for many it will be difficult to receive the sacraments because of public persecution, now is the time to cherish the sacraments. 'I am the bread of life', said My Son, and He is in the sacraments. *'He shall enter that hears these words and does My will.'* As My Son said this, I tell you go now and read the gospels and live these words, do My will and frequent the sacraments and you shall enter, My children.

Come to Me, hear My warnings, I long to be with you."

8th June, 1993.

187 "The moment, it is all you have. The next moment belongs to Me and as yet I have not entrusted it to you, so concentrate on the moment you are living. When you are with people you must give yourself to them for that moment, for I am in those people. *If you give them only half your attention you give Me only half your attention.* If you give them cold charity you do the same to Me. Love them, all people, that is how you love Me. Half measures are not for souls in love, give everything.

The moment is so important because now is when I need My work done in millions of little ways. And if you continue to do My will in the little things you will learn how to say yes to Me, your God, and should I ask anything greater then you will be prepared.

Yes, is the word you should say to Me when the Spirit prompts you. No, is the word you should say to the devil when he tempts you. Each day will be a series of 'Yeses' and 'Nos'. You must direct the yes always towards Me.

Ask yourself before saying yes to anything, Does this or will this please God? And if you want to love Me more ask yourself, Can I love God and please God more by saying No to this, even though there is nothing wrong with it?

Mortification My children is essential. Say no to all that food that your bodies don't need. Deny your appetites and you will grow more and more in love with Me.

The act of denying yourself the luxuries is beautiful and brings Me much joy, and I give you many graces for doing so, but you must struggle to perfect your mortification by specifying the intention for which you are mortifying yourself. Because then, I can direct the distribution of My graces more effectively.

My children you must learn to say 'no' to the world. It will lead you astray. Just because you can have, doesn't mean you should. Mortify yourselves and you will never lose your taste. *It is by sacrifice that love grows strong and this is how you will keep your savour. You are the salt of the earth My children.* You are entrusted with the task of adding flavour to the world, the taste of My Son's precious body and blood."

8th June, 1993.

188 "My son, don't worry about the future just give Me your whole self now, that is all you have to give. Tomorrow does not belong to you yet. (.....)

One day at a time, give Me the day and you will come to the end of your life having given Me your life. (.....)

The only way for you to go, if you desire true happiness, is My way. My way is full of thorns and roses but My love will get you through. Protect and defend at all cost the love of Me in your soul. I your God am dwelling in your heart, don't let Satan demolish My home.

You must struggle with the people around you who irritate you. You must be full of love for everyone. (.....)

Above all, be happy, but always let your outward conduct reflect the peace of your soul, and always in your devotion to Me, let your conduct be like that of a soul in love, which you are. What I am saying My son is, you don't have to be afraid of what you are. Be a man of prayer, be a man of the sacraments, be a man of sacrifice, it's all part of being a man of Christ.

(.....) Never walk out on a bad note and never cause an argument that can be avoided, and it can be avoided if there is not a moral issue involved.

(.....) Day by day My child, fear not, I am walking with you. (.....) I will be your loving support at all times. Rest with Me My child."

9th June, 1993.

189 "No matter your age, no matter your state in life, these messages can help you to grow closer to Me, your Heavenly Father, and do My will in everything you do. My children today I speak to you all, men and women, young and old, priests, religious, and laity. I have chosen this young boy in the middle of nowhere to receive My messages and I have entrusted to him the mission of spreading the messages.

These words are from wisdom itself. I am God-I am wisdom. You must have faith in these messages and live them out. They don't oppose the church; they support the church; they support the Pope especially. And these messages are directly linked to the work John Paul II, (the chosen Pope for these times) has been entrusted with.

My children accept this boy into your homes, support his cause, for I am the Lord your God.

My children return to the sacraments and return to living lives of prayer.

I have spoken to this young boy so that he can share it with all of My children. I am the Lord your God; I have used an extraordinary way to bring you back to the ordinary things of your faith, like the sacraments and prayer.

My children I love you all and My delight is in being with you. Receive these words, they are *'Words from God,'* but more than that, you must all start to live these messages.

Now is the time, you are the person, and change is the need. Soften your heart today so that you can love Me more.

Read, believe and live."

9th June, 1993.

190 "People of God, act like it. Abandon all your pagan practises and offer to God all those things that you can.

In society pagan practises and rituals have taken over especially in the area of gift giving and special days.

Return to putting emphasis on feast days. On special feast days celebrate in your homes with special foods.

On Christmas Day make Christ the centre, send cards that depict the real importance of Christmas, the birth of My Son, Jesus Christ.

Don't give eggs so much at Easter as celebrate and appreciate what you receive that day as the fruits of My Son's passion and death.

On any day when you eat, bless the food before you begin, whether you be in your home, in a park, or in a restaurant. If you love Me you will not leave Me at home, you will take Me wherever you go.

It is time that followers of Christ started to live their faith publicly, not by any showing so that people admire you or otherwise, but because this encourages your brothers and sisters in the faith to do likewise.

At work have a small crucifix on your desk, or a picture of Mary: this will also help you to spread the faith. People will ask, what is that? And then you can say that you are a Catholic and they will see that you stand for something, that you believe in something.

Then through your words and actions you must show people that you try to live out what you believe.

Never gossip, it is destroying much of My children's work. Work hard to avoid gossiping and stop others from gossiping when you are there. Is it that hard to change the topic?

If someone says something that is morally wrong, speak out, say something, it is your duty.

You are living in pagan times My children avoid becoming like pagans yourself. Be what you are, sons and daughters of God. Make them feel uncomfortable if that is what it takes, and you will probably feel uncomfortable too. But, love them and if you love them you will want to bring them to Me, so they can enjoy My love too.

Above all remember, you are followers of Christ, so you must carry the cross. Don't change your lives, keep doing what you are doing unless it is immoral, but go into the middle of the world and live out your faith in every activity.

You will change people like this, you will sow the seeds of conversion, you may not be the one to reap, but remember, some sow and some reap.

Today sow the seeds of conversion. Stop being lost amongst the pagans. Live your faith and you will be spreading My message, in many cases without even opening your mouth.

But above all, don't be afraid to speak out. Defend Christ. He has been crucified for you, the least you can do is defend Him with words."

10th June, 1993.

191 "Sincerity, Integrity and Honesty. Today My children examine yourselves in these areas. Are you sincere in your dealings whether personal or professional? Do you maintain an exceptional level of integrity in your personal dealings as well as your professional dealings? Are you honest, even

when it hurts your pride or costs you dollars?

These "words" are just that, words, in society today. Bring them back as values and standards in your personal and professional lives. If you can attain and sustain such attributes you will be doing My work, but forget not, that part of most of My work is carrying the cross.

The cost of My work here for many will be professional outcasting and personal loss of acquaintances. Move on to bigger things professionally, give more time to your friends who appreciate your honesty, and never forget that I, your Heavenly Father, am with you.

Bring values and standards back into professional and personal dealings and little by little people will begin to realise the importance of My love. My children today bring the other children along with you to enjoy My love."

10th June, 1993.

192 "Death. Those who love Me and live in My love are not afraid of it, and struggle to keep themselves ever ready for it.

Death My children, more in these times than in any other times, is like a thief that comes in the night, you know not when and you know not why.

For the faithful death is just a train ride to life with Me. But to the faithless millions, death is something to be avoided at all costs, something of great concern and something horribly feared by most.

Rest in My love now and remember all I have told you through the gospels and the Church's teachings and you will come to believe that death is a beautiful thing. Love Me and the day you die will be the most joyous of your existence.

When others around you die, pray for them. If people are growing old and remain faithless, pray that they are enlightened by Me one more time before they die.

For all I give many opportunities to respond to My grace, but many still do not. Many cut themselves off from My grace through mortal sin. When you go to funerals pray for your own souls as well. Meditate on the reality of death so that you may always be prepared.

I tell you today My children, the devil is not a myth, he is real and roams the world destroying souls that let him. Those souls join him in the hellfire. The fire in hell is worse than all the fires that have ever been lit on earth put together.

Here on earth it is possible for people to endure, sometimes quite happily the non-presence of Me, God, in their souls. They try to seek happiness and peace in temporal things. But after you die My children you will see things as they really are.

Those who are away from Me will know, without any shadow of a doubt what they are lacking as a soul disunited from Me.

The pain of not living in Me is worse than all the fires on earth. A soul in love on earth that falls into mortal sin aches painfully, this is mild. The pain is horrendous. *If a person could experience it completely on earth it would kill the person instantly.*

My children today I am warning you of the reality of life apart from Me after you die. You must seek to be saved.

All those who hear the words of My Son, Jesus Christ, and do My will, they shall be saved.

Children, don't be foolish, respond to My merciful warnings."

11th June, 1993.

193 "Children, how innocent and pure of heart they are. That is how I want you all to be. Society has robbed you and most of your brothers and sisters of your innocence many years

ago. And as innocence disappears your heart is contaminated with muck and your heart becomes impure.

If your heart is full of this muck today, return to My love, come to confession, make a good confession and try to keep your heart pure from then.

Don't look at girls in ways that you would not want your mother or sister looked at, and the same goes for girls, with their father and brother.

Dress cleanly and properly and above all do not rob young children of their innocence. Don't swear and particularly don't blaspheme. Don't watch unsavoury television programmes and in all circumstances control your imagination.

Children is what you must all try to be again. You cannot erase images and ideas from your memories automatically, but every time something that is offensive to Me, your Heavenly Father, enters your mind, kick it out. Address Satan and you will extinguish all the unsavoury memories of your broken innocence.

You must struggle to keep your heart pure, for what a man says and does comes from his heart. He whose heart is clean and pure, he shall see the kingdom of Heaven.

To those who destroy innocence in young children, I tell you today, the weight on your shoulders is huge and the chains on your legs unbearable to any human. Renounce your wrong doings and change paths, come and work for Me to sustain innocence in the young people of today.

This is a mission I entrust to all of you My children. Sustain the innocent minds and pure hearts of the young. Don't let them be exposed to the indecency that is rampant in society, and above all pray that you may work untiringly to make your heart pure, and for young people that they may maintain their innocence.

Of all the human qualities and virtues, innocence is one that pleases Me very, very much."

11th June, 1993.

194 "I tell you My children, not one stone will move out of place if it is not part of My plan. My plan is beautiful, My kingdom will reign on earth as it does in Heaven. Prepare for the coming of the Lord.

All of you must straighten your paths now. I sent John the Baptist to call people to do the same and now I send these words of warning, encouragement, and guidance, to tell the world to repent, to change their ways for the second coming is at hand.

Before too long My Kingdom will reign on earth, Satan will be defeated once and for all, and My chosen people will live in the harmony of My love.

From anything that is bad I extract good, and you can see how much bad is all around you. Don't dwell on it and become depressed, think of all the good that I will extract from all this bad.

I will give you a sign of My coming back into the world: There will be many natural disasters, some will wipe out whole cities, even whole nations. People will suffer greatly, whether they belong to the world or to Me.

Many will ignore My warnings, many will go to hell. You must pray and work hard to save souls. Ask Jesus My Son and Mary My daughter to help you to spare you and to spare your family and friends. *I have entrusted all My graces to Mary in these times, and her Son Jesus will be much pleased if you persist in prayer to and with her.*

Don't worry My children, like a father cuddles his children in the night when a thunder storm is raging, so will I cuddle you in My love during these end times. At all times you must remember I am always with you and trust in Me your Heavenly Father."

12th June, 1993.

195 "Your message is simple: love. Your job is to teach the world about love, real love. The world does not know how to love.

Bring them to Me My children for I love all men, bring them to Me and by My love I will teach them to love.

Life is love. If you don't love you don't live. Love is like the soul breathing. If your body doesn't breath you will die. Those who don't love, their souls will not know life. A soul can never die, but to know true life it must come to Me, and the only way to Me is through My Son Jesus Christ. And He is love.

When Christ was on earth, He showed you how to love. As a child, as a young man, as a son. Can you not learn so much from Christ?

My children Christ is your example. Many of you, in fact most of you are called to live lives like Jesus did for the first thirty years of His life. But a few of you are called to live lives spreading His message, like the last three years of His life.

Regardless of which way of life I call you to, there are two main things that are shared and that you must keep firm in your mind always: love and the Cross.

You are all called to love and the way to love is by carrying the cross.

Never think like the world does with respect to love, because it isn't easy to love, it's very difficult, it costs, it is forever a new challenge, and you never, ever really perfect your love.

Finally My children, you are nothing. So all that you do is to be attributed to Me your Heavenly Father for I am goodness. And I am all the goodness that is in, and that comes from you.

As you are nothing, I must be what makes you great. And I give you one more strength to rely on. Mary, Mother, Daughter, and Spouse of God. Without her none of your efforts will be fruitful, I suggest you seek recourse to her often.

Gather My people in My love."

12th June, 1993.

196 "You are still so young. Even the oldest of you have only lived a fraction of your life. For I am life. Come today and reflect on Me, your God, as life. And how do I give you this life? In the Blessed Eucharist.

Present in the Eucharist is the Body, Blood, Soul and Divinity of your Lord Jesus Christ, My Son.

So many of you search for life in this world, but in the wrong places. And many of you grow old and still your hunger is not quenched and you wonder why not. It is because I am life. And the way you come to Me is through My Son Jesus Christ. The life you are looking for is in the Blessed Eucharist.

On this, the feast of Corpus Christi, reflect on the privilege you have of receiving true life. Then if you reflect on the beauty of this mystery then you will want to frequent the Sacrament more often. *And you say you don't have time: make time, and I will multiply the effectiveness of all your other work.*

Pray today that the world starts to receive the Blessed Eucharist. So many people around you are in the state of mortal sin when they receive the Blessed Eucharist.

You must all learn. Study what the church teaches, because if you don't study these things, your faith and apostolate will not be as strong as they could be. It is essential that you have the facts because this knowledge will overflow into your apostolate and make it ever more fruitful.

I am your God, does anyone else deserve more respect than I? When you receive Me in the Blessed Eucharist prepare yourselves well. When you are in Holy Mass rise above the human element to realise that I am there. Help others, by acting correctly. Genuflect in a manly way, unless you are unable.

And above all guard your churches against the wrong types of change. The Eucharist is the centre of the Mass, do not allow anyone to move the tabernacle, it should always be in the centre. Don't take the kneelers out of the Church. Be on your knees for the consecration.

Adore the Blessed Eucharist with profound reverence."

13th June, 1993.

198 "Come to Me My children and live in My love. Let Me fill you with the fruits of My peace and joy. Let Me touch your hearts so that you can love again.

Today My children I invite you to daily Mass. Start slowly, one extra day, then two extra days, before long you will come everyday. You will hunger for My precious body and blood.

My children it is by the Mass that you will learn to live. Because to live you have to suffer. The Mass is a sacrifice, in the Mass you are taught about the suffering that My Son Christ endured.

Don't hesitate when suffering comes your way, accept it lovingly in My name and offer it to Me for the conversion of sinners.

Do you not see My children, the Eucharist will change the world. Of all the many gifts I have given you, the Mass and the Eucharist is the greatest. You have the opportunity everyday to attend, if you can come.

And if you want to, you can. *I will multiply your time if you are generous with your time with Me.* Today and each day from now, come and receive My Son's precious Body and Blood, the bread of life."

14th June, 1993.

199 " (....) This is how it is. The end times are near, but this does not mean the world will end. No, after these end times and during them many will be returning to My love. *The harvest will be great, but the labourers will be few.*"

14th June, 1993.

200 "My children, do I ignore you? No, then stop ignoring Me! During the Mass I lay up here on the altar in the broken body of My Son and I am ignored.

How can you ignore the broken body of your Saviour who is lying on the altar in front of you.

Reflect today on the real presence of Christ in the host, and remember where the Son is so is the Father. Think about His blood and how it was shed on Calvary. It is not enough just to receive. You must receive and believe, to live. If you don't believe, you put up a barrier to My life, supernatural life.

My children you are body and soul and you have a duty to feed both. The best food for the soul is the body and blood of your Saviour and Lord Jesus Christ, but you must accept it worthily and knowledgeably. To accept it worthily you must be in the state of grace. To accept it knowledgeably you must understand, and acknowledge, and believe, that My Son Jesus Christ's body, blood, soul and divinity are present in that host.

It is only by recognising what really takes place in Mass that you can obtain the full benefits, My children. If you don't understand the importance of the Eucharist, read, there are good books.

Ignorance must be overcome My children, you are chosen to bring the world back to My love: and the way is by the Eucharist.

Make the Eucharist the centre of your lives and all will be well."

15th June, 1993.

204 "I am the centre of everything. Make Me the centre of your lives. Make Me the centre of everything you do. Give up everything of self, abandon all to Me, your Heavenly Father, so that My will can be done on earth as it is in Heaven."

16th June, 1993.

206 "To all of you today My children, I say this, you are all part of the one body. Your task is one. Your mission is one. Your journey is one.

Some of you will be priests, but this does not mean that all of you should not be part of My priesthood. All of you are called to spread My Word. Priests are called to be other Christ's, in a ministerial vocation, but you are called to spread My word.

For too long society has said, "That's the priest's job." Now you must all begin to realise that if together we are to unite the world as one in Christ's name, then you must all work together: priests; religious; and, laity. Your task is one, your mission is one. *Join nations at the seams with Christ's love.*

You were born to be saints, My children. Personal sanctity is a goal that should be very firmly implanted in your mind, but the salvation of other souls is essential and your personal sanctity depends upon it.

You must all struggle in your place in the world to let Christ reign. In your homes, in the office, you must particularly struggle in the churches because there are many who are blindly taking the glory and honour that belong to Christ away from Him.

These end times are calling for a joint task undertaken by priests, religious and laity, and that task is to sustain and preserve the Catholic truths.

I'll say it now and be warned, women were not created to be priests.

To women, young and old, I say this, learn the beauty of being treated like a lady, being treated well and looked after by men. Then demand it from all men around you. Furthermore, learn the beauty of life in the home, this is your place, your role is child birth and for special chosen ones your role is solely a life of prayer in religious vocation.

Don't let men treat you badly. Demand what is good and proper.

And to men, young and old, now is the time when you must restore the dignity of a woman's role at home.

Together you are one flock and in the end you will be lead by one shepherd, when My Son's glorious reign comes. And then, in the name of Jesus Christ the world will be returned to it's intended glory, one community, one message, one task: to seek and love the will of God."

17th June, 1993.

208 "Children, come now and follow My Son Jesus, for the way He leads you, leads to Me.

The cross is large and heavy, cold and harsh, but the fruits of the cross are eternal. Coldness can fade in an instant, be removed by a heater. Life, in the cross, lasts eternally.

Children, be children of the cross, gather together to form one body. I tell you this, those who work hard in their Father's work will find a place in Heaven.

Go now into the fields, the harvest is ready, the harvest is great. (.....)

And then when the time is right you will bring in a big catch. But even with big catches, the fish swim into the net one by one, each being caught up in the net of My love in a different way. *Each soul deserves individual attention.* What is gained quickly is lost quickly.

As the days, months and years go by your boats will often be too small and you will have to call your friends in other boats to help you with the catch and you will need new boats. My plan is perfect, don't worry about the temporal, take care of the supernatural, your personal sanctity is primary to everything else.

The harvest is great but the labourers are few. Gather My labourers My child and go and work in My fields.

Carry My Son's cross, you have never known such joyful pain. Keep firm in your mind always that the pain of this life is temporary and the joy of living in My love, is eternal."

18th June, 1993.

209 "My child, life on this earth is like the blink of the eye. And that is why I say to you, seek only My will and all else will be accounted for. On this, the feast of the Sacred Heart of Jesus you all need a heart transplant. Come now take your hearts and transplant them into Heaven.

To do this you need a few words that constantly recur in your day: What is God's will for me now? If you ask yourself this often throughout the day, in everything you do, then your heart will be in Heaven. He that loves Me, seeks and does My will.

I your Heavenly Father will always give you the graces necessary to carry out My will. And the way these graces come to you are from the Sacred Heart of Jesus, through the

Immaculate Heart of Mary.

Pray that you might grow to know and love the two witnesses better, because under their direction and guidance you will find Me.

The all inclusive part of doing My will, is the cross.

The cross My children, I talk to you often about it, but you never really understand. With your heart you must love the cross.

And the way to Me, your Heavenly Father, is through My Son Jesus Christ and only then by the cross.

So, if your heart is so important in relation to the cross, and the cross is so important to your individual salvation, do you not see that you need to guard your heart.

Yes, place locks on your hearts, seven or more, so that your heart will always belong to Me. If one breaks repair it.

Keep your heart under lock and chain in case you become attached to something of this world not intended for you, it could cost you salvation."

18th June, 1993.

210 "My children, today I invite you to learn more about your Catholic Faith. If you are to sustain the truths of the Catholic Church through these end times, you must know them. You must read and study. (.....)

Do you know the commandments? Do you know the main precepts of the Church? Are you a Catholic? If you are, then you should be living your Faith, and you cannot live it if you don't know what it is.

So many of you, My children, suffer from scrupulous attacks from the devil simply because you don't know a certain point of your Catholic Faith. The basic Catholic truths were not given to you at school, so now is the time for you to learn about them.

Together gather and discuss them. Discuss the commandments and the precepts of the Church. Discuss their relevance, complete relevance to life in the twentieth and twenty-first centuries. It is only by a group of people knowing and living the true faith that it will be sustained and preserved.
(.....)"

19th June, 1993.

212 "Let your light so shine before the world so that on seeing your good deeds your neighbour will give praise to God.

This world is walking in darkness. They have forgotten how to believe, remind them My children; Faith comes from hearing, but if no one proclaims the word of God, by works and actions, then the unbelievers don't hear *God's message*.

Stop living your faith behind closed doors. Take Christ into your workplace, take Christ everywhere you go, and that is how the unbelievers will hear His words and learn to believe.

It is not enough to attend Mass and to pray. At baptism each of you received the mission of apostolate, of spreading the faith. My children spread the faith.

Go out and proclaim the words of God, speak socially about different aspects of your faith, discuss problems you have with certain articles of doctrine, but always consult the Church's teachings in this case. And get someone to explain why the Church teaches what She teaches. It is so natural what the Church teaches.

Take yourself away from those earthly attachments and you will discover the real beauty of your faith and you will grasp Catholic doctrine and take it to heart, and make a home in your heart for it.

Detach yourselves from the world, learn more about your faith, proclaim My Son's message, and you will start to truly live your faith. Your heart will rejoice and sing the praises of the Lord."

20th June, 1993.

213 "Don't allow those around you to drag you from My Will. It is not enough just to do My Will at your leisure, or when it pleases someone around you, do My Will now. Whatever I ask of you My children should be done as rapidly as is humanly possible, without delay, unless your prayer reflects otherwise.

You must all become docile to the promptings of the Holy Spirit, especially in prayer. Pray My children, ask that the Will of God may be revealed to you. Ask through the Son and He will plead at My right hand, and through the Holy Spirit I will send you the discernment of My Will.

If you pray, you will know what it is I am asking of you in the moment, for that day, or vocationally. Pray, because unless you pray and discover My Will, your hearts will be restless.

The 'Will of God' is all that you need concern yourself with. In prayer, ask for anything you want, need, or desire, but always conclude as My Son Jesus Christ did, 'Not my will, but your will be done, Father.'

I am the Lord your God, I have a beautiful plan, for the world and for each individual, trust in Me, I know what is most beneficial for your souls, children.

Live in constant search of the 'Will of God' and then you will find favour with Me your Heavenly Father. 'He that hears the words of My Father and does His will, he shall enter'. My children, listen to Jesus."

20th June, 1993.

214 Mary: "My children you must begin to live these words from God. I am your Mother and I watch over all but there is only so much I can do, and if you turn away from Me you not only cut yourself off from My help, but also from the graces that God so willingly bestows on you. More than this, you offend your Heavenly Father very much if you abandon Me.

So believe these messages, live these messages and pray the Rosary. Trust My children, Trust."

20th June, 1993.

215 "Today My children let us discuss charity. Charity begins at home. Love your family. And all charity begins with prayer. So what I am saying is pray for your families. If they are away from the Church, pray that they return, and offer sacrifices that they return and do good works for them and for your neighbours, that they might receive the merits from God for those works.

Charity is not just giving money. Charity is denying self. Charity is a selfless stand, often hidden, for the benefit of another person or people.

The world is distorted on its view of charity. Write a cheque: that's easy. But no, first pray and then act. Anything that is not done with your hearts and minds lifted to God, is worthless in the eyes of God.

Today My children I call you to learn to pray first, lift your hearts and minds up to My Heavenly altar and make an offering that the world cannot see, and then go and do all you can by human means to support this good cause, or assist your neighbour.

Charity is empty and cold unless you invite Me to join you. All charity comes from Me your God. Today children pray with love, from your hearts, and the fruits of this prayer will be charity."

21st June, 1993.

216 "You lack character My children, you see all about you things that appal you, yet you remain silent. Have I not given you tongues and the gift of speech? Then speak. If not out aloud against the offence, then quietly in your heart speak to Me your Heavenly Father and apologise for their offences against Me. By this you will win merits for yourself and merits for others which will lead to their conversions.

Quite simply you need to form solid Christ-like characters. Be like Christ. *Your mere presence should be enough to signal that certain types of behaviour and conversations are not acceptable.*

You must live the gospel in the middle of the world in the 1990's. By the year 2000 many will be converted to My love, but My plan is reliant on you My children, to each play your individual roles.

You are called today to accept My words and live in My love. Many have rejected My love, and many will. They will feel the whole force of Heaven against them when fires come from Heaven, when My justice comes to those who abuse their freedom, which has been entrusted to them by Me your Heavenly Father, so that they may pursue eternal happiness for their souls and assist others in doing the same.

Today My children, pray about your characters. (.....) Does your outward conduct reflect the existence of My word in your heart?

If My word hasn't a place in your heart, fear not, build a home today in your heart for My word. Five or ten minutes a day is all it takes. Then pray, because strength of character comes from prayer. In prayer you solidify the food given to you through the gospel. In prayer you make the word a part of you. By My grace, in prayer you make your character strong. Pray My children, nothing I tell you, nothing, is more important."

21st June, 1993.

217 "The great chastisement will come to the homosexuals as well as other gay communities. Those countries who maintain communist rule will suffer greatly. And 'advanced' nations who are unsympathetic to poorer nations will also feel the wrath of My justice."

218 "My children if only you knew what your reward will be like if you do My will. If you knew you would most definitely live My Holy Will every moment of the day. It would still be a struggle and many would still fall, but they would get up.

The devil has tried to remove all traces of union with Me from the world, he has been unsuccessful thus far, but don't be fools, the devil never sleeps and he won't give up until the last. He won't give up until the heel of the woman clothed with the sun crushes him.

Today My children I call you to seek union with Me in this life through Prayer, Mass, Confession, Fasting, the Rosary. And then this union will be much greater than you could even imagine in Heaven, after this life of yours.

Stay where you are in the world, the devil will try to convince you to leave the world. Don't. I need you right where you are. I need you to do My work there. Ask yourself: If I leave, who will do my Father's work in this environment? Very often you will be the person for the job. Don't run away from the world. Don't let yourselves be dragged away by the devil. Hold firm and trust in Me, the Lord your God, I will comfort you and give you rest.

My children, you are called to live as apostles in the middle of the world. You must not get into the habit of speaking to those only who will comfort you in your faith. *You all have a duty to spread the faith.* You must introduce people slowly to My love. You cannot operate always on your level. The only way to win apostles for Me is to show them that you understand where they are at. You must go to their level of understanding; you cannot start talking about miracles if they don't know the basics of the faith or their belief will be shallow and more than often you will get a cold response.

Be warm, be understanding, be gentle, be humble, be prudent, be calm and remember no one can harm your soul. Do what you have to do then, be an apostle, spread the faith. *Unless My children remain in the middle of the world My plan will not come to fruition. Your goal: To do the will of God. Do as I ask, My children."*

22nd June, 1993.

219 "Today I come to speak to you about parties and music. Parties, as I have said before, are an oasis of sin for the devil. You must all learn how to have clean, wholesome, Christ centred fun.

When you have a party, or go to a party, there are many virtues needed. Firstly modesty. Be modest in appearance and in the way you act. Prudence. Be prudent in the way you encounter all people and avoid situations or environments that might lead you away from Me, your Heavenly Father. This may mean not going to a particular party at all.

And above all you must have fortitude. In case something unexpected happens you must have the armour of fortitude ready. Do what you have to do when you have to do it.

You must live Holy Purity. Don't let your eyes wander everywhere. Be master of your body. Control where you look and where you don't look. Prudence helps you to live Holy Purity.

Don't over eat or drink. Gluttony is a forerunner for impurity.

Be clean and chaste at parties, in words thoughts and actions. You all must help each other, don't make it difficult for each other.

Have parties where the environment is good. And above all whatever the environment, don't abandon Me, your Heavenly Father, for I am always by your side to guide and protect. I am your strength in the face of temptation: live the presence of God.

Secondly, music is a powerful tool. It is a psychological instrument being used to the greatest levels by Satan. Don't listen to the radio. Select carefully what you listen to and do not listen to anything too often. Learn to appreciate one off listenings to music, this puts up a barrier to the effect it can have on you.

Don't be fools and think, 'I'm strong I can handle it', it effects everyone. You are human, you are weak. And wasn't the first sin a sin of pride?"

22nd June, 1993.

220 "Direction. You all need direction My children. The one who tries to steer himself is heading straight for shipwreck.

My children pick out someone you know and trust and who has access to the answers. See the person regularly, he will direct you to see what it is God is asking of you.

Then you must trust this person. Be docile to this person. *The greatest reward in Heaven is given to the obedient.*

Listen to the promptings of the Spirit as this person offers you advice. Don't turn away because you don't like what you hear. Could it be that it is so true that it repulses you? Be a man, face yourself, then act. Do something about it.

One change at a time and you will change the man that lives inside that wretched body of yours. You will be a man of God before long with the right direction.

You ask: How do I know who to pick? The answer is this: Pick someone who wants for nothing else but the will of God.

My children it is through others that I will speak to most of you. (.....)."

23rd June, 1993.

221 "Surely if for the path you have chosen you expect criticism then you will try even harder to be fruitful.

I am the vine and you are the branches. You are branches of Mine, My children. Be fruitful. All My branches are fruitful. They serve other branches. They sway in the wind at first, but as time goes by they grow thick and stern, so no gust of wind, which is only momentary, can destroy a lifetime's work.

It is like this with you too My children. You will be judged by the way you stand up to the winds of this world and you will be judged by your fruits. My branches are fruitful and you are My branches, but be fruitful. You need the sap from the trunk and roots to be fruitful. I tell you, you need prayer and the sacraments.

If any of your apostolic activity is to be fruitful it will be an overflow of your interior life. That what is in a man's heart is what he speaks of.

Today reflect on the importance of prayer, because this is the preparation of your branch for fruit. You will be fruitful if you pray My children. And all persecution will be falsely founded if you remain humble, and the fruits of your branch will be the proof. The proof that you have come to spread the truth. The words of your Heavenly Father."

23rd June, 1993.

222 "You are naturally lazy and weak. You are human. Raise your hearts and minds to Me your God for a few moments now and make resolution to do a few things each day that will establish order in your days.

Firstly get out of bed at a fixed time, on time, everyday. Don't be lazy, start the day off well. Then, set a fixed time for your mental prayer everyday. Next set a fixed time to retire in the evenings. With these three set, your focus should be on Me, your Heavenly Father and your time will multiply.

If you want to really love me, My children, you need order."

24th June, 1993.

223 "Children, Do you think I put you in the world to run away from it? No, you belong in the world, but not to the world. My children you belong to Me, your Heavenly Father.

Don't quit your jobs, or leave your Universities before many days of prayer. I am not saying stay on forever. Stay on until you become aware of what My will is for you.

As children of God you should want for nothing else but the will of God.

Keep nothing for yourselves, give it all up. And there in your prayer, day by day, will piece together the beautiful plan I have for you. I will lead you step by step. Do not be afraid, I am with you.

You have no need for security, I will be your security. The security this world advocates is a myth and is momentary, incomplete. My security lasts for your lifetime and for eternity.

During these end times you must seek My will, and try to obey the promptings of the Spirit.

I am the Lord your God, he who does My will by keeping My commandments and living My word, he shall enter.

Children, do not fret if you don't know where it is you are going. Before long, if you pray you will see clearly. But always remember you will see only what you need to see for the short term. In the long term trust in Me.

And don't run away from the world. *It is in the middle of the world that you must do My work.* Carry My Cross. Please!"

24th June, 1993.

224 "My children, today you must learn not to discard all that you don't understand as being wrong.

If you don't understand something pray for the light of faith. Faith will let you understand. Quite often your lack of understanding is not because of your lack of knowledge, but your lack of faith.

Ask for faith My children and through the Spirit I will enkindle the fire of faith in your hearts.

Believe My children, but not blindly.

There are many different movements within My Church. All are not for everybody. If one doesn't appeal particularly to your way of thinking do not ridicule or stand against it. Spend your time proclaiming the truth.

If you are concerned that something is not coming from Me, your God, take this attitude: 'If it is from God who am I to stand in His way. And if it is not from God, it will go away.' Do not waste your time and energy which belong to God, trying to bring other religious movements down.

Your time and energy should be devoted to proclaiming the truth. The one and only Catholic Truth.

My children as you stand alongside these messages you

yourselves will be abused and ridiculed, your reward will be great in Heaven.

My children keep strong in your faith. Be full of Hope. And ever consistent in your charity. You will be known by your fruits all over the world and you will be fruitful. Be patient and trust in God."

25th June, 1993.

225 "Reach out to the lepers of the world and touch them. You are unable to heal the physical illnesses in the world, but don't you see, they are minor.

The lepers are those poor souls living in sin. Those people in pointless pain because they don't know My Son.

Where is the social justice? So many people are heading along the devil's path.

You My children are the doctors of these souls. Concern yourselves with the heart of their problem. Have concern for their souls. The rest will be taken care of by My divine providence.

Serve My children. Serve the sick. Serve souls.

Your job is to bring souls back to Me. Salvation of souls: keep it firm in your mind always."

25th June, 1993.

226 "I am with you My child."

26th June, 1993.

227 "Be perfect as your Heavenly Father is perfect, My children. You look as though you are content with your spiritual status. This only indicates that you need yet another conversion. You must never be content, strive for perfection.

I'll give you a little secret: if you want to be perfect, you must be simple. Of course you will never reach a state of perfection. But by struggling to achieve perfection all your life you will reach your goal: union with Me, your Heavenly Father.

Perfection is found in simplicity. You are poor wretched human beings, if you would only realise this you would make the devil's job that much harder.

Then be simple. Do simple things. Write simple things. If you want to be perfect, you must practise perfection. By practising doing something poorly you will never perfect it. Do it well. Aim for perfection.

You must be ruthlessly efficient if you are to do My work well. I have much planned for each of you My children. I am just waiting for each of you to individually respond to My call."

26th June, 1993.

229 "My children your personal sanctity is all you need concern yourself with. (.....)

In time you will see that from the beginning I had given you everything necessary to do My will, and more, because I will set the Spirit free within you and He shall work through you to show others how to do My will.

One, Holy, Catholic ambition: Do the will of God. Repeat it often in your mind and to others. All else will come if you do this."

26th June, 1993.

230 "My children, hunger for the truth and you will be happy. I will be your happiness. For too long corruption, watered down truths and mistruths have been ruling society.

Look at the legal system, it is not just. Justice is a word misused, but I the Lord your God, I am just.

You must all begin to reflect on the gospels daily. Then you will learn of the truth. And the truth will set you free.

If you do this well, My words will come and make a home in your heart and it is then that you will live My word.

If you don't know My word how can you live it. You must read the gospels daily. The truth is in the gospels. My Son is in the gospels. Justice is in the gospels. Life is in the gospels. My love is in the gospels.

The way is through the gospels."

27th June, 1993.

231 "Children, be in love. I want you to love Me. I want you to fall in love with Me, so that I can show you the way to life.

Life is more than a living cell, for a human being. For a human being life is about loving Me the Lord your God. It is only then that you can live life to the fullest.

You have so many human attachments and they are keeping you from Me. Throw away all of that, *leave everything behind and come and follow Me.* You will never regret it.

My love is greater than all the human love put together. I can love you like you have never been loved before. And I long to love you more and more, so tear down the barriers to My love.

My children, be good children. A good child is obedient and loving. But more than that, a good child wants to do what his father wants of him. A good child is cheerfully obedient.

Don't feel disgruntled by your knowledge of Me and My absolute justice. Be comforted by My absolute mercy.

I am the Lord your God and I long for the day when together we will share My Heavenly mansion, but until that day you must gather My sheep. You must work in the fields for the harvest is great but the labourers are few.

You are My labourers and all men will know you as holy men and women of God. As, the labourers of God."

27th June, 1993.

232 "My children, your individual mission is all you should concern yourselves with primarily. And what is that mission: You must be saints!

Unless you aspire to be holy men of God then all your apostolic activities will be fruitless. You were born to be saints. Now is the time, if you have not already, to join the road to sanctity. *If only you knew the delight I take in My saints, just men in the middle of the world. You should never underestimate the lengths I will go to, to help one such man.*

I am the Lord your God and you are My children. Be good children, do as your Father asks and your Father will see to it that you have everything that you need.

Go now and work in My fields. Many of you will have dual occupations. All will work in My fields and as well as this many of you will spread throughout the professions of the world. Many will be labourers in a more earthly sense. I tell you it is the labourer in the sun all day who raises his heart, mind, and work to My Heavenly altar that brings new meaning to the word hope.

Your hope must be simple. And your love must be simple. Work and work hard. Offer it to Me your God and that will lead you to sanctity. Hope in the future. Visualise that everyone will be offering their work to Me your Heavenly Father. How beautiful the world would be.

Pray now My children, pray for all souls and slowly one by one gather the great harvest. Bring people back to My love. My children, enjoy the day and please labour hard in My fields time is scarce."

28th June, 1993.

233 "Must I tell you again My children, you must focus on loving Me in the moment. Do you not have all you need for now, and even for a week to come? Then no need to worry, you have eight days to work hard and pray hard so that what you need on the ninth will be yours.

I am the Lord your God, none of My children will die of hunger. I will give you a place to rest your head and I will clothe you with all the magnificence of a spring morning.

Don't hesitate for security's sake, trust in My divine providence and all will be well. I will provide.

My children I wish to speak today about hard work and divine providence. The two rely on each other. I will not drop money out of the sky. (.....) If you don't go to work I cannot pay you.

For all My children I want this: a stable job that demands of the individual and sound spiritual development. For some the later will lead to a full time job in My fields. But for most both will be essential.

Don't leave your jobs. You need to work hard so that you can support yourselves. You need money. You need to live on planet earth and to do that you need money. Don't despise the world for I your Heavenly Father made it.

You will always need money even after these end times. So find yourselves good jobs that serve well and pay well.

Do what it is I am asking of you no matter how hard it is for you. Some jobs are hard and seem useless and of no supernatural value. If you have that view, first go and work, now, before you do anything, and learn to lift your heart and mind to Me in that work. This is a sure way of being lead to your vocation."

28th June, 1993.

234 "My dear children it is so urgent that you respond to My call with a complete love. Keep nothing for yourselves, give everything to Me and I will give it all back to you and more.

I will give like you have never received, to those who place their trust in Me. Your Heavenly Father's love is like a light that burns forever acknowledging the presence of truth. You must put this love in your hearts so that you can bear witness to the truth My children.

Today, My children pray. Pray about your weaknesses, bring them to Me and I will make you strong.

It is I the Lord your God who makes the strong and I will surely make My own children strong. In Me lies your strength, without Me you have no strength.

Come now and drink of the thirst quenching waters of My love and you will have strength to last the whole day through."

29th June, 1993.

235 "And on this rock I will build My Church. And I have. My Church dates back to Peter. The One, Holy, Catholic, and Apostolic Church. And now the head of My Church is John Paul II, a great man.

My children, the Church will always be. I will protect My Church. I will provide the people, in fact, among you are some of the people, and they will see that the truths of Catholic faith are delivered from these end times. They will ensure that Catholicism lives forever and that My Church never dies.

These end times will be very difficult for the labourers of

God. Don't despair. People will come and go, but with them they will take fragments of the truth. Others will come and stay and sustain and preserve the truths of Catholicism in their entirety.

Children you must long to be saints. Yes, you must long to join Me in Heaven after your life on earth.

It is up to you to work in My fields and My fields are the normal streets and alleys of your lives.

Peter was the rock on which I have built My Church. Paul converted many to a love of Me. It is here that you receive your mission. Align yourselves with the truths of the Catholic Church and preach to all who need to hear My words.

Tell all to repent. Don't contain your preaching to the converted. (.....)"

29th June, 1993.

236 "Children, you must be the ones who stand out. If you live the human and theological virtues even to the tinniest degree you will be noticed as followers of Christ, as children of God. It does not take much to be noticed in the world today.

Don't shy away from living your faith in a noble manner when others are around. Focus on Me always. Don't worry about what others will think. Don't try to impress them by your prayerful posture, if you are praying they will notice. Put Me at the centre, and My will, will prevail.

Children run around now in the playground and make new friends. It is by friendship that you will crush all hatred. Do not give anyone reason to count you as an enemy. You must befriend all men, but you must be honest, while prudent.

You must carry the cross in the area of friendship, many will not understand. They will say you are not the person you once were. Fear not, follow firmly along your way, the way that you know is right. The reason they don't recognise you is because it is no longer you that lives, but Christ that lives in you.

Don't hesitate, you know your path, now follow with the energy that a sensualist craves for pleasure. You must endure the heat the world gives off. You must prepare yourselves interiorly.

My children, Pray, Fast, go to Mass and regular Confession, say the Rosary, and make your mortification as constant as you breath.

Do My will children and all will be yours."

30th June, 1993.

237 "Stop to consider, today, the value of one soul. My children, the graces that I pour onto each and every soul are uncountable. The soul that goes to hell doesn't want to be saved. This soul has picked self over Me, the Lord your God.

Don't think that you will border on pass or fail. The difference between going to Heaven and going to hell is great. There is no mistaking the soul destined for Heaven. This soul is very different to that which is set for hellfire. But My children, My point here is that I can see clearly and complete-ly into the souls of all My children, but you cannot. Thou shalt not judge.

Today My children you must learn to treat all equally. Male, female, young, old, black, white, are all the same. See with new eyes today and all you will see is souls rejoicing in My love.

See each person as a soul but do not judge. And love all as souls. Love all as you love Me."

30th June, 1993.

238 "How little time it takes, spent with Me, to fill you with zeal for all of your apostolic activities. My children to love Me, to follow My Son, you must pray.

Go today and sit in front of a tabernacle and speak to My Son Jesus. Tell Him about all your worries and fears and He will remove all your anxieties. Tell Him about your plans for the day and the joys and problems you expect to encounter. Too many of you only tell Us of problems. Many beautiful things are happening, share them with Us in prayer. Speak to Us about everything that is happening in your lives. As your friend We want to know.

In Jesus Christ I gave you the perfect example. Did He not teach you how to pray? And so, I continue the lesson now.

Speak to Me your Father, to Jesus My Son, and to the Holy Spirit, but especially to Jesus in the tabernacle. It is then that you will know Our love."

1st July, 1993.

239 "What are you going to do with your lives? My children, each of you has a particular vocation. Take time out each day and you will hear Me calling you. Often it will feel like I am dragging you in a direction you would rather not go. But it is not until you get there and resign to do My will that you realise it is in My plan for you that you find the only real happiness on this earth.

One of the reasons for these messages is that young people, and not so young people, might reflect on them and by doing this and living the messages be led to their vocations.

Many young people are scared by the mention of the word vocation, simply because they think too much might be asked of them. My children whatever task I ask of you, I give you sufficient graces to do your task tremendously well.

Others are scared that they will be dragged away from

married life. The greatest dignity that I can bestow on a man is to be a priest. If I call a man to be a priest, that man was picked from the beginning of time for that task.

Children, you must pray about your vocations. Ask Me for light and I will give it. And Sacrifice, make sacrifices so that you might have more light as to your vocation.

I will lead you. I am with you. Trust in Me the Lord your God."

1st July, 1993.

240 "Children, let nothing concern you. Around you are many souls, young and old, who will twist and turn like snakes at the sight of you, just as you have, and do, at the sight of others who show you the way.

And why do people behave like this, because a little light has been shone on the darkness of the person. And the person sees room for improvement, the person sees an opportunity to love Me more, but instead wants to hold something back for himself.

Give everything to Me then you will be truly happy. Give until you are empty, then, and only then I will be your fill.

Today My children I call you to look more at yourselves, instead of continually gazing at the weaknesses of others.

Ask yourselves: What am I holding back from God? Ask yourselves: How can I love God more?

So many of you spend so much time working out how you can love Me the least and get into Heaven. This is not the way, surrender, abandon yourselves to Me. Do everything you can to love Me. You can never do enough.

Love Me and I will shine upon you the love of My divine mercy."

2nd July, 1993.

241 "Examine yourself. Do you invite other people to share with you the beauty of your faith. How long is it since you invited someone to a prayer group, (.....) or to join you at a weekday Mass, or to say a Rosary in the car on the way to your destination.

At Baptism apart from sanctifying grace you receive a mission. And that mission: to spread the faith.

Come out of your comfortable, closed environments today My children and extend a welcome to all those who are in need of your welcome. Ask them to join you, the worst they can do is say no. Don't be a coward. Put your shoulders on the cross My friend.

It is not a member's club restricted to the elite few. *The beauty of Catholicism is every human being's right.* Ignorance is an evil in so many ways and prevents the spread of faith. But what is worse are those people who accept ignorance. And worse than that still are those who have the truth and don't allow others to escape their ignorance by spreading the truth.

My children you have nothing to be ashamed of, live your faith. You must be active in your faith and you must be actively living out your apostolic mission.

Remember, don't rush souls, they take time. Gently invite others to join you at various events pertaining to the Love of Me, your Heavenly Father, good wholesome Catholic events.

Go out today as apostles of Christ."
2nd July, 1993.

242 "If you really want to love Me, you will do as I ask.

Don't take these words for granted My children, you must respond to them. You must let the Spirit change the way you live your lives. It is time to take a stand on the principles of the Catholic faith. Live what you believe, but first, discover the true beauty of what you believe by reading and studying about your Catholic faith.

My children you have to get to know Me, your Heavenly Father. And you ask how: I am in the Son and the Son is in Me. If you have seen the Son you have seen the Father. Get to know Jesus Christ.

I want you all to give Me your whole lives whether I am calling you to married, single, or religious life. I want you to give everything to Me. If you are going to give your life away you want to make sure you know whom you are giving it to.

If you look into the beauty of your faith your hearts will be unchained from the world and then you will want to give them all to Me, your Heavenly Father.

If you are to help souls you first need to grow in love of Me yourselves. Unless what's in your heart is love of Me you will not show others how to love Me. All your apostolic activity will be an overflow of your interior life. And interior life allows Christ to come and live in you more. So do you see that by working on, and improving your interior life, your ability to bring others to the faith will grow. Why? Because it will no longer be you that lives but Christ that lives in you."

3rd July, 1993.

243 "Forgiveness. Today My children look at Me your Heavenly Father and learn about how I forgive all who repent. And then learn to forgive as your Heavenly Father forgives.

If you live My will then without doubt many will trespass against you. Don't waste your time trying to justify yourselves. Simply go about your ways in peace and harmony and turn the other cheek to all those who care to disrupt My will. Don't let them disrupt My plan, get on with your work. And cry to Me, 'Forgive them Father for they know not what they do.'

Forgiveness comes from Heaven. I want for all My children

to join Me in Heaven, and My divine mercy in My forgiveness reflects this. And yet so many run from Me, so many ignore My call to return and ask for My forgiveness. If there is sorrow in your heart, there will be forgiveness.

My children you must convey the compassion I have for all My children. Let the world know that I the Lord your God am kind and merciful."

3rd July, 1993.

244 "Appreciate the gifts I have given you. My children you don't seem to understand the many great gifts I have given you. Could it be that you are still too caught up in yourselves?

Today reflect only on one gift. The gift of My Son, Jesus Christ. If you can grasp the significance of this gift your life will take on a whole new meaning. If you have grasped it before, recollect what you have previously discovered, and then go off again with the same zeal you did the first time you discovered it.

And what is it about, this gift that is so important to all human beings: by His death He destroyed your death and by His resurrection He raised each of you to eternal life.

Supernatural outlook is what you need to appreciate this truth. There is life beyond the grave. Life isn't a game to see who can own the most, or earn the most, or have the most pleasure.

All that you are My children comes from Me, your Heavenly Father. I gave you all your talents and abilities. I gave you all the faculties that allow you to enjoy pleasure.

And why do you think I gave them to you? I gave them to you so that you could have eternal life. I gave them to you as means of your sanctification. My children, you were born to be saints!

However, My children, I gave you freedom to do as you will,

when you will. And many of you, in fact all of you, use that to offend Me through sin.

Today I call you again to do My will. Appreciate the gifts I have given you and the reason I have given them to you. Then grasp the responsibility that comes with freedom and show Me that you love Me by hearing My words and responding to them."

4th July, 1993.

245 "Day in day out, the same things and you tell Me that it all becomes so monotonous and that you feel tied down. The problem is you have little love. You must grow in love and then the repetition in your days will be beautiful and you will not feel tied down, you will feel immersed in My love.

My children you must all bring a little more order into your lives, especially you, My son. It is not enough to love Me when you feel like it. Your love for Me must be consistent. You must do little things in the day that bring you to raise your hearts and minds to Me your Heavenly Father.

My children you must pray everyday . Mental prayer is essential for sanctity in these times, as is the Rosary.

Not monotony, Love."

4th July, 1993.

246 Mary: "My children I am the breath of fresh air in the new day. I am the light sent forth to remove all darkness. I am your Mother Mary, Queen of peace, and peace is what I want for all My children. May the peace of the Lord be with you always.

My children don't let anything take this peace away from your souls. As persecution begins to mount you must keep firm in your mind your aim: to do the will of God, so as to achieve your sanctification.

I am your Mother, Queen of Heaven, I will bring you all you need. You have an abundance of human qualities already My children, take care of spiritual matters and do everything you can in temporal matters, and leave the rest up to Me. My children, I will bring to you all you need, just keep firm in your path to do God's will."

4th July, 1993.

247 "Wherever you go you live in the presence of the Mass. Think occasionally, when things go well, or something goes badly, that somewhere in the world Mass is being said and you are receiving the fruits and graces of that Mass. Is that not beautiful?

Today My children try to develop your understanding of the significance, (and the benefits that come to the Church) of the Blessed Eucharist, which is the body and blood of your Lord Jesus Christ.

Consider the effect each Mass has on Catholic souls throughout the world. Consider the effect public adoration has on souls throughout the world as well as souls in purgatory. And more than these, public adoration gives souls the strength of fortitude, those present in a special way, but those all around the world.

Come My children and adore My Son in the Blessed Host. My children it is here that you will find the strength to do what it is I am asking of you.

Today My children My plea is that you adore the Sacred Host on the altar."

5th July, 1993.

248 "If all you ever do is listen to those who call to you along your way, 'fool, you're wasting your time,' then you will be holding up My plan. Pray for those people. Then move on and help those who are willing to respond to My call through you, there are many millions of souls who need help.

My children to you all I say this, do My will. Don't let anyone or anything distract you, get on with the job.

Place firmly in your minds what task I am asking of you then with ruthless efficiency set about doing it.

It is in My will that you will be greatly persecuted, but it will be in My will that you find your greatest joys.

There are always critics and sceptics. Ignore them if they claim atheism, listen if they align themselves with My Church. Then weigh up what they say, pray, adjust your course if need be. Then put your head down and continue zealously along your way."

5th July, 1993.

249 "My children today I wish to speak to you about hope. This is the theological virtue that allows you to move on despite worldly setbacks, armed with the weapon of faith.

Hope is beautiful and so childlike. And you all must be children. I am your Heavenly Father and I hear all your cries for help. Hope in Me, have hope in Heaven, and live a good and virtuous life.

If you don't live good and virtuous lives you kill the virtue of hope. You may maintain a facade of having faith, but hope is lost to worldly worries.

Have faith in My Divine Providence and then trust in Me your Heavenly Father and I will show you the way step by step. And then when you put all your trust in Me, you will discover the true beauty of hope.

Today My children live in hope of Heaven, trusting in Me

your loving Father and I will look after you in your lifetime. I will give you all you need. My children, those who trust have hope. And those who have hope have been enlightened to realise there is something to hope for. Your job is to help Me enlighten more souls. No one lights a lamp and puts it under a bed.

I have put a light in your soul, don't put it under the bed. Live your faith, express your hope in the way you act, the decisions you make, and that way other souls will be enlightened.

You are a light set on a hill for the world."

6th July, 1993.

250 "If you are going to do My work you need formation My children. Read the messages, reflect on them and the Catholic truths will slowly filter through to your soul. Read the gospels, so that you can learn to be like Christ, and pray the Rosary, so that you can learn of the humility and love of your Mother. Pray and sacrifice constantly. Every chore and every joy should be a prayer. Sacrifice is often the most heart felt prayer. It is here that you show Me so often how much you love Me.

My children your intelligence draws you to My love and to love Me. But your lower animal faculties drag you away from Me because of original sin. You must learn by will and by sacrifice to master your lower faculties, so that you can love Me more.

To love Me is to harmonise the natural with the supernatural. And you must know Me to love Me. If you want to know Me and what it is I ask of you, then it is important that you read these messages and pray about their contents. *These words are of My own especially for these times in the world.* To ignore these words would be to reject My Divine Mercy. If you love Me, you will hear My words and do My will."

6th July, 1993.

251 "As the years go by you will all grow in love of Me and you will look back at your past and see the times you have offended Me, you must not let this play on your mind and get you down.

I am your loving Father, I forgive and I forget. You are human and so you cannot understand this. *Don't limit Me, your God, to the scope of your intelligence.*

Don't judge yourselves My children. Go to confession regularly and do small sacrifices consistently, and struggle against temptation. I am not unreasonable; this is all I ask of you.

Consider the moment at hand and the future, they are the only times that can further the glory you receive in Heaven. Those who struggle to achieve sanctity as outlined in these messages will receive a very high degree of glory in Heaven. Woe to you unbelievers who disregard these messages as a young boy's mental illness, you will feel My wrath of justice on the last day. Woe to you who hear these words of Mine and carry on selfishly as though you were never exposed to My infinite Mercy. It is a wicked society that demands a greater sign than words straight from My mouth, the Lord your God.

There is only one way to Heaven and that is through My Son Jesus. If you have read these messages you will be aware that there is not a new message, but Christ's message repeated. My children you were born to be saints and this calls for constant change.

So today resolve that the future will be different. Then give this moment to Me, do My will. Ask yourself: What does God want Me to do now? Then without hesitation, do it. This is how you will achieve sanctity. In the tiny moments of the day.

For very few of you have I planned large spectacular events and ways of loving Me. Most of you must learn to love Me through the ordinary events and works of each day.

Be My children. Respond to My merciful call. Do My will. For My house has many rooms and My greatest desire is to have you living with Me in My home."

7th July, 1993.

252 "Children, Children, gather round close. My love is infinite. I am love, and I want to share it with you for eternity in Heaven.

But first you must live your lives on earth amongst the wickedness and snares of the devil. Believe in Me and he is powerless. He cannot make you do anything and I always give you the power, by grace, to conquer.

You were born to be saints My children. You were born to be children of light. You were born to give glory and honour to Me, your God. My children, you are to be children of the truth. And I am truth. Surrender yourselves to My will. Zealously seek My will in everything you do.

You ask Me how will you know My will. The answer: pray. With prayer anything is possible. Carry My cross and you will see with clear detail My will at any given moment.

You are called to be apostles of the truth. My apostles, sent to a world so lost and confused. And in this world there are many flocks of sheep and for each I will send a shepherd.

Fear not My dear children, I will send you a 'good shepherd'.

Follow My Son, Christ. He will show you the way to Me. Concern yourselves not with the things of this world but with the life everlasting. And you must all help others to see in these terms as well.

Pray for your friends and family that they might learn to see the importance of their one nature: body and soul.

My children, you must show interest and compassion for all My children. You must show concern for every soul. Out of one hundred souls you are interested in one hundred.

However, do not spread yourselves too thin. Help the few that you can and that will set in place a multiplier effect.

The harvest is great, but the labourers are few My children. Please gather the harvest for Me by spreading the truth. This unbelieving world is thirsty for truth but ignorant as to its source. Show people the source of all truth.

Many are caught up in self, don't worry they will see. In fact, the time is coming when you will all see with the eyes of your soul the truth about the way you live. And then people will hunger more than ever for the truths of the Catholic faith. Prepare yourselves My children by studying and reading. You must be able to speak of solid doctrine. You need to tell them more than the last miracle that has happened.

You ask Me why I am speaking to you, this is why: The truth needs to be preserved and sustained through these end times. Many manifestations of the Holy Spirit are taking place, but people are responding in the wrong ways.

These happenings are to direct you back to the true faith, but instead people are becoming caught up in all these miracles. More and more people are calling for miracles: it is a wicked nation that demands a sign. Even after I, or Mary, Mother of God, grant a sign, they still respond in the wrong way.

The only way to prepare for these end times is by personal sanctification. You must all aim to be saints. This is My will for each and everyone of you.

You must pray, sacrifice, go to regular confession and communion, say the Rosary, read good spiritual material to develop your understanding of the basic doctrines of the

Church, do charitable works, and love all souls as they were Me, the Lord your God.

This is the only preparation for the times that await at the doorstep of the world.

My son tell the world to pray and return to the sacraments. I am the Lord your God, I come to you out of My infinite mercy in these words, but before long I will come to you out of My infinite justice and the world will feel the wrath of My justice through natural disasters worse than those ever experienced. Now is the time to respond My children.

Seek My will in each moment and live not for pleasure in this life but in hope of Heaven.

Seek first the Kingdom of God and His justice and all else will be given in addition.

My children, spread these messages, deny no one the opportunity to hear My warning one more time.

I have spoken to this young boy, but I speak to you all, he is merely the instrument I have chosen to use.

These messages are to each and everyone of My children throughout the world. These messages will show you how to live My will in the midst of these times."

7th July, 1993.